THE ANCIENT PATHS

by
Craig Hill

FAMILY FOUNDATIONS PUBLISHING
P.O. Box 320
Littleton, CO 80160
Website: www.familyfi.org

Family Foundations Publishing
P.O. Box 320
Littleton, Colorado 80160

Cover design by
DB & Associates Design Group, Inc.
P.O. Box 52756
Tulsa, Oklahoma 74152

Printed in the United States of America

All scripture quotations, not otherwise noted, appear in The New American
Standard Bible. The following versions have also been used: *The New
American Standard Bible,* The Lockman Foundation, 1960, 1962, 1963,
1968, 1971, 1973, 1975; *King James Version*, Thomas Nelson, Inc.,
Publishers; *The Amplified Bible,* Zondervan Bible Publishers, 1965, 12th
Printing, 1975.

*The characters in many of the examples cited in this book are real life
people whom the author has known. For their privacy, however, their
names and some of the insignificant details have been altered. Alternatively,
some incidents described are not sequential events, but are composites of
several incidents, nevertheless, they reflect very real situations.*

CONTENTS:

DEDICATION:

To my wife Jan, and two sons Joshua and Jonathan. I praise God for the treasure of their company in waling along the Ancient Paths.

SPECIAL THANKS TO:

Dr. John Bradshaw, Kim Clement, John and Paula Sandford, Gary Smalley, John Stocker, Dr. John Trent and Dr. Sandra Wilson whose teaching deepened my understanding of The Ancient Paths.

Vonnie Hill, my mother for editing.

Earl and Margie McAvoy for typesetting and graphics.

Chapter 1
ASK FOR THE ANCIENT PATHS

One day while reading through my Bible, my attention was drawn to the following peculiar scripture as being important:

> *"Thus says the Lord, 'Stand by the ways and see and ask for the ancient paths, where the good way is, and walk in it; and you shall find rest for your souls.' But they said, 'We will not walk in it.'"*   *Jeremiah 6:16*

As I began meditating on this verse, I wondered what the Lord meant by *"the ancient paths"*. Here we are directed to ask for the *"ancient paths"*. The first thing I did in my investigation of the passage was to look up the Hebrew word for *"ancient"* to discover its meanings. I found that the Hebrew word is *"**OLAM**"*. Some of the meanings of this Hebrew word are: old, concealed, hidden, perpetual, eternal, timeless, from eternity.[1]

When I read the words *"from eternity"*, something inside me jumped, and I remembered reading in the Bible how everything on the earth is patterned after things in heaven. The things on the earth are really just types and shadows of the things in heaven. God's ways are heavenly, eternal, timeless. Before God created man or the earth, His ways were established, and He walked in them. When God created Adam and Eve, He made them in His own image and established within them His ways: supernatural, timeless, from eternity. These were ways of thinking, ways of speaking, ways of behaving and relating to one another. Since man chose sin, he has departed farther and farther from these ways. Today we don't even recognize what "*these ways*" are any more, so we couldn't return to them if we wanted to do so.

Nevertheless, God instructs us through the prophet Jeremiah to see and ask for the "*ancient paths*" again. He tells us that they are the "*good way.*" The Hebrew word for "***GOOD***" used in this passage is the word "***TOV.***" Some of the meanings of this word are: pleasant, agreeable, happy, well-off, prosperous, great, excellent, cheerful, merry, distinguished[2]. Such characteristics are the result of walking in the ancient paths of God. This scripture passage further says that when you walk in these paths, you will find rest for your soul. So many people today have very little rest or peace on the inside. Life is a constant struggle, and there is a continual torment on the inside of many. God never intended for us to have to live this way. Such a state is not walking in "*the ancient paths.*"

When God created man and placed him on the earth, He made him in His own image and programmed him with His own ways. Since that time, man has departed farther and farther from the original ways of God. Even after sin entered the world, man still lived 900 years. By the time of Noah the life span of man had already decreased to around 600 years, while in Moses' day men lived only 120 years. Today the average life span is about only 80 years. The farther away from the original ways of God man has departed, the shorter his life span has become, and the more complicated he has made his own life.

SUPERNATURAL POWER JUMP

As I continued to meditate upon this passage of scripture from Jeremiah, the Lord reminded me of a physical principle which I had once studied in a college physics class. Everyone knows that the high tension power lines that stretch across our country carry high voltage electricity. Electrical power from these lines can be accessed by physically connecting a conductive wire to these lines. However, few people know that electrical power can be induced in a conductor wire that is simply stretched parallel to an active electric line without the conductor wire's touching the line or being physically connected to it in any way. By simply being stretched parallel to a set of electric lines, a copper wire may conduct electric power right through the air with no physical connection whatsoever. On the other hand, a copper wire stretched perpendicular to electric lines will not conduct any power at all. Electrical power line workers have been electrocuted when not understanding this vital principle.

Even as electrical power jumps across free air to a parallel conductor wire, so God's supernatural power and life can jump from Him to you when your ways are lined up parallel to His ways. The only problem is that we don't know what God's ways are so that we might line up our lives parallel with them.

God originally established His ways in culture so that they would be imparted naturally from one generation to the next. In my study of several different cultures of the world, I have concluded that God has established a significant deposit of His eternal ways within virtually every culture of the world. When God's ways are established within any given culture, there is no need for a specific intellectual knowledge of these ways. However, when God's ways are systematically eliminated from a given culture over a few generations, then the people within that culture *"perish for lack of such knowledge."* (Hosea 4:6)

In our North American culture, over the last several generations, people have decided that we don't have to think, behave, or do things "that way" any more, so that now we honestly don't know what "that way" is. Consequently, the Lord admonishes us: When we once again find God's ancient ways and begin to line up our lives and families accordingly, we will begin to experience a supernatural jump of God's life and power into our lives.

SUPERFICIAL HEALING

"For from the least of them even to the greatest of them, everyone is greedy for gain, and from the prophet even to the priest everyone deals falsely. And they have healed the brokenness of My people superficially, saying, `Peace, peace,' but there is no peace. Were they ashamed because of the abomination they have done? They were not even ashamed at all; they did not even know how to blush. Therefore they shall fall among those who fall; at the time that I punish them, they shall be cast down," says the Lord. Thus says the Lord, "Stand by the ways and see and ask for the ancient paths, where the good way is, and walk in it; and you shall find

> *rest for your souls. But they said, 'We will not walk in it.'"* Jcrcmiah 6:13-16

These verses, immediately preceding verse 16 of Jeremiah 6, give us some further insight into our present experience of life here in North America. Because we have not walked in God's ancient paths, many areas of our society, as well as personal and family life, seem almost overwhelming on a daily basis. Consequently, important spiritual, emotional, financial, family, and health needs seem to go unmet day after day. As a result, as verse 13 tells us, we become very self-focused and greedy after gain. When his/her needs go unmet, a person tends to become selfish and greedy. It is impossible to tell a drowning man not to be so greedy for air, or a starving man not to steal for food. As verse 13 tells us, greed and deceit are bound to operate when crucial needs go unmet.

Verse 14 states that we are not helping people when we, the church, attempt to bring healing to the brokenness of people in a superficial way. Perhaps we have thought we were helping people through speaking *"peace, peace"*, thus attempting to remove their guilt and pain without dealing with the root causes of their problems.

People in the 1990's are interested in instant solutions to problems. I have often thought that a drive-through church would probably be very popular. I could see people pulling up to the drive-through window on Sunday morning and ordering: "one order of McHealing, three McSalvations, two McDeliverances and one McSermon to go, please." We are an impatient society which, by and large, is unwilling to deal with root causes of problems; we want only instant pain alleviation. As a result, many times we go through life daily making choices aimed at just eliminating the painful consequences of our last foolish choice. We rarely look far enough ahead to see the longer-term consequences of the choices we make.

SHORT-TERM FIXES ARE ALWAYS THE SEED OF LONG-TERM DESTRUCTION.

Suppose a teenage girl who has been deeply wounded and alienated from her father enters into rebellion and cuts off relationship with him. She has now stepped outside the circle of spiritual protection which God designed in the family for her safety. Having been deeply wounded and hurt by her father, the young girl now goes out in search of love. Suppose she meets a young man who says that he loves her. Because of the hurt and need in her life, she allows herself to become sexually involved with him, resulting in an unwanted pregnancy. Unfortunately, her second, foolish, short-term choice of sexual satisfaction has resulted in a longer term consequence. Pressured by an unwanted pregnancy, this young woman makes a third, foolish, short-term choice by deciding to abort her baby. This action results in the long-term consequence of untold guilt and shame at having taken a life. The torment and hurt of this situation then result in a new quest for comfort and love. Another romantic relationship is entered, and again an unwanted pregnancy occurs. However, still carrying the tormenting guilt and hurt from the previous abortion, the young woman chooses this time to have her baby. She begins to pressure the father to marry her, and eventually he does.

Each choice that this young woman makes is designed to attempt only to remove the pressure of the consequence of the last short-sighted choice. After only a little time of being married, the young woman discovers that the man she has married is full of anger and very abusive. As a result, after a year she chooses to divorce her husband. Still carrying tremendous hurt and pain from the rejection from her father, the abortion, the second unwanted pregnancy, the abuse of her husband, and now the divorce, she once again sets out on a quest for love and comfort. You can probably play out the rest of the scenario yourself in a string of broken relationships and devastatingly painful events.

Verse 15 of Jeremiah chapter 6 tells us that when we make short-sighted choices attempting to bring peace without dealing with the roots of the former wrong choices, we harden our own hearts and are not even convicted of any wrongdoing. Jeremiah says that when men do this, they don't even know how to blush. This hardening of heart then becomes the very cause for their downfall and destruction. This is why Jeremiah in verse 16 urges us to seek after and ask for the *"ancient paths"* where the *"good way"* is.

MERCEDES VS. MACHETE

"But they will say, `It's hopeless! For we are going to follow our own plans, and each of us will act according to the stubbornness of his evil heart.' Therefore thus says the Lord, `Ask now among the nations, who ever heard the like of

this?   The virgin of Israel has done a most appalling thing. Does the snow of Lebanon forsake the rock of the open country? Or is the cold flowing water from a foreign land ever snatched away? For My people have forgotten Me. They burn incense to worthless gods and they have stumbled from their ways, from the ancient paths to walk in bypaths, not on a highway,"   Jeremiah 18:12-15.

In this passage, Jeremiah is again urging us to return to the ways of God. He states that forgetting God is as foolhardy as turning away from the only source of fresh water in a desert land. In verse 15 the prophet tells us that when we don't walk in God's *"ancient paths"*, we are walking in *"bypaths."* When I first read this passage, I could picture a man attempting to cut his way through a thick jungle with a machete in order to get from point A to point B. The distance was quite vast, and it looked as though it might take the man most of his life to progress to the goal.

On the other hand, verse 15 says that the *"ancient paths"* are like a super expressway. I could picture another man also moving from point A to point B. However, rather than hacking his way through a jungle with a machete, he was riding in a Mercedes Benz on a super highway. The second man in the Mercedes was able to reach in one day the same goal that it took the first man with the machete all his lifetime to reach. If we will just stand in the way, see and ask for the *"ancient paths,"* and begin to walk in them again, I believe that we will find ourselves riding on a highway instead of slowly cutting a path through the jungle in many areas of our lives and society. Daniel 11:32 tells us: *"But the people who know their God will be strong and do exploits."*

Most of us have not had any time to do any exploits, because we are caught up in a survival mode. When we have to spend most of our time cutting through underbrush and fending off wild beasts, we have no time to do anything other than just survive.

When thinking of evangelism and expanding the Kingdom of God, I had always heard that each generation is responsible to evangelize its own generation. As I pondered this one day, I began to wonder who is responsible to evangelize my children and grandchildren. Of course, I concluded that this also is my responsibility. However, over the last couple of generations we have had to evangelize in each generation the children of the previous generation of Christians. We have had to set up coffee houses and street ministries to win back to the Lord the children of Christians. Why? We have thought that if we just take our kids to church, pray for them, teach them the Bible, or even put them in a Christian school, then they will grow up to serve the Lord. However, experience has proven to us that although all these things are valuable, in and of themselves, they do not adequately set the course for life.

What then is necessary to set a course in the lives of Christian young people which results in their serving Jesus Christ all the days of their lives? I believe that the answer to this question has to do with an impartation of two key qualities from the Lord at crucial times in life. In every culture God established His ancient ways of instilling these key qualities at important times in the lives of

9

children. However, in our culture here in North America, we have forsaken and forgotten God's ancient ways and, as a result, have failed to receive in our own lives or to impart to our children these two key qualities.

Walking in God's ancient ways results in generational evangelism. Each generation is responsible not only to evangelize its own generation, but really to evangelize at least two generations ahead. If we again rediscover God's *"ancient paths"* and begin to walk in them, we will virtually ensure that our children and grandchildren will serve Jesus Christ all the days of their lives.

Let us now move on to examine the two key qualities which God intended to impart and establish powerfully in each of our lives: **IDENTITY AND DESTINY.**

---

[1] James Strong, "The Exhaustive Concordance of the Bible," Abingdon Press, New York 1890.
[2] IBID.

Chapter 2
IDENTITY AND DESTINY

Whether we realize it or not, every day every one of us answers two critical questions. 1) **Who am I?** and 2) **Where am I going?** We answer these questions based upon preexisting images already established deep inside. How we have answered these questions determines the way we respond to life's circumstances.

The first question, "Who am I?" pertains to what we will call **IDENTITY**. Identity very simply stated is my perception of me. The primary issue at stake in dealing with identity is **VALUE**: "What am I worth?" So when we speak about identity, we are speaking about my perception of myself and the value of my life and being.

The second question, "Where am I going?" pertains to **DESTINY**. Destiny has to do with my perception of my function and significance on this earth. The primary issue at stake in dealing with destiny is **PURPOSE:** "Why am I here? What am I supposed to do?" Identity and destiny are key qualities which God intended for us to have correctly imparted and established in all of our lives. The course for our adult lives is set through this impartation of identity and destiny which we receive while growing up as children.

"Finally be strong in the Lord, and in the strength of His might. Put on the full armor of God that you may be able to stand firm against the schemes of the devil. For our struggle is not against flesh and blood but against the rulers, against the powers, against the world forces of this darkness,

11

*against the spiritual forces of wickedness in
the heavenly places."*   Ephesians 6:10-12

Whenever I used to read this passage of scripture, I
thought that it taught that we were to stand firm against
the devil.   However, one day the word **SCHEMES**
jumped off the page at me.   I realized that we are not
fighting against just the devil himself but against his
schemes. I began to wonder exactly what a scheme is and
how to stand against it.

Every good manager knows that in order to govern
people effectively, he must set up management systems
that run themselves.   The president of General Motors
cannot personally supervise every assembly line worker.
Have you ever thought of the fact that Satan and demonic
spirits don't multiply?   However, people do.   Therefore,
the same number of demonic spirits is operative on the
earth today as was 100 years ago when there were only 1
billion people. Today there are over 5 billion people. If
Satan is going to manage his kingdom of darkness with a
constant number of demons, but an ever increasing human
population, he is going to have to set up management
schemes that run themselves.   Neither Satan nor even his
demonic   hosts   can   personally   afflict   each   person
continuously.

The first thing we must learn from this Ephesians 6
passage, is that we are in a spiritual battle. Many of us
have read the evangelistic tract, "The Four Spiritual
Laws." The first law stated is that God loves us and has a
wonderful plan for our lives. We could draw a corollary
from Ephesians 6 which would state that the devil hates us
and has a terrible plan for our lives. Whether we like it or

not, we find ourselves in a spiritual battle. It is the devil's purpose to set up schemes in our lives and in society that run themselves to bring about destruction with or without our awareness.

In returning to the concepts of identity and destiny, I stated that how you answer the questions, "Who am I?" and "Where am I going?" in childhood will set a course for your adult life. It is the purpose of both God and the devil to provide you with the answers to these key questions. If Satan is able to establish his images of identity and destiny in your life, he then has set up a system of governing your life that more or less runs itself and requires very little maintenance or service on his part. It is an effective scheme of destruction in your life.

I believe that it has always been God's intention to impart, especially at specific junctures in life, His message of identity and destiny. He has appointed special agents on this earth to ensure that His message of identity and destiny is revealed. These agents are called **PARENTS**. Their primary job is to make sure that children receive God's message of identity and destiny throughout their growing-up years. Satan's purpose is to access these very agents of God, the parents, and to impart his message of identity and destiny. Many times parents are unwittingly used to impart the devil's message rather than God's.

SATAN'S MESSAGE VS. GOD'S MESSAGE

What type of message does the devil want to reveal regarding identity and destiny? His message is something along these lines. **IDENTITY**: "You are worthless. You aren't even supposed to be here. You are a mistake.

13

Something is drastically wrong with you. You are a 'nobody.'" **DESTINY**: "You have no purpose. You are a total failure. You'll never be a success. You are inadequate. You are not equipped to accomplish the job. Nothing ever works out for you, etc.."

I once heard a woman say, "It's as if someone dropped me off on the planet forty some years ago, and I've been trying to make my way the best I could ever since. But deep inside, I don't feel as though I belong here, and I've been waiting for that someone to come back and pick me up." God never intended for anyone to feel that he doesn't belong. That is Satan's message.

God's message of identity and destiny is something like this:

IDENTITY: "To Me you are very valuable and are worth the life of Jesus Christ. You are a `somebody.' You <u>do</u> belong here. Before the foundation of the earth, I planned for you. You were no mistake."

DESTINY: "You are destined to a great purpose on this earth. I placed you here for a purpose. You are a success as a person and are completely adequate and suited to carry out My purpose. Set your vision high, and allow Me to complete great accomplishments in your life."

JOE'S STORY

Joe was a well dressed, successful business man in his late thirties when I first met him. He had come to a weekend *"FROM CURSE TO BLESSING"* seminar. As we moved into the small-group ministry time, Joe began to share, somewhat sheepishly, about the tremendous problem that anger had caused him in his life. "Anger causes me to embarrass myself, and then I feel guilty," he explained. "One time a couple of months ago I was driving my car out of a shopping mall parking lot into a stream of traffic. I thought that I had enough space to exit the parking lot and enter the traffic flow on the street. However, as I began to move my car forward, I suddenly realized that I really didn't have enough space between cars to enter. So after moving just a few feet, I stopped my car and decided to wait for a larger space in traffic. The man in the car behind me was apparently surprised and gave me a little toot on his horn." Joe went on to describe, "I was so infuriated that he would honk at me, I slammed the gear shift into 'park,' and jumped out of my car, almost ripping the door off the hinges on the way. I stormed back to the car following me, grabbed the shirt of the startled driver and jerked his face up through the open window. I then let loose a tirade of choice obscenities and profanity as I let him know what I thought of him. All the time while screaming at the other driver, it was all I could do to restrain myself from physically punching him."

"When I had exhausted my vocabulary of four-letter words and felt that the other man sufficiently understood how I felt about his honking, I returned to my car. As I sank back down into the driver's seat, tremendous guilt and shame began to overwhelm me. I almost felt as if it had been someone else shouting those words. 'Who was that crazy, raging maniac?' I thought to myself. 'What a wonderful testimony of the love of Christ I presented to that man following me!' Then I remembered the bumper sticker that my wife had recently attached to the back bumper of both our cars, 'Honk if you love Jesus.' I just sank into a pit of shame and depression all the way home." Joe continued, "Not only that, but sometimes I get so angry at my wife that I am afraid one day I'm going to physically strike her. We have a two-year-old son, and when he cries and wakes me up at night, I get so angry that often I just have to get out of the house and go take a walk, or I'm afraid I might hurt him, too. I've prayed and prayed to get rid of this anger. I've repented of anger. I hate it. I've told God that I'll do anything to get rid of it, but nothing seems to work. It's ruining my life and my marriage," he said with exasperation.

I suggested to Joe and his wife that we pray and ask the Holy Spirit to reveal to him the root cause of the anger in his life. He agreed, so we began to pray. Simply asking the Lord to show Joe anything that was pertinent to his anger, we quietly waited. After a few minutes, I asked Joe, "Well, did the Lord show you anything?"

"No," he replied, "nothing pertinent."

"What came to your mind?" I queried.

"Oh, just a dumb experience I had years ago when I was a kid," he said. "As a matter of fact, I hadn't even remembered that experience until now, but it doesn't have anything to do with my life at this time."

I urged Joe to share about the experience, but he continued to maintain that it wasn't pertinent. Finally I told him, "We asked the Holy Spirit to reveal to you anything He wanted that was important, and this experience was the only thing that came to your mind. So why don't we just trust God that He was reminding you of that experience for a reason, and perhaps we will discover that it is relevant."

I have found that many times when people have been deeply wounded and hurt in their lives, through the impartation of the devil's message of identity and/or destiny, especially by parents and other key individuals, the pain is so great that it is buried deep inside and never really dealt with. Because of the intensity of the pain, many times a key experience is even blocked entirely from the memory, and when it is brought to the surface, the individual is not at all in touch with the emotional pain still down deep inside from that experience.

As a result, regarding such memories or experiences, people will often times say things such as, "Oh, I've dealt with that" or "I forgave my dad a long time ago for that" or "Oh, that doesn't hurt any more." Christians will often say, "Oh, I've put that under the Blood." However, many times the pain has not been released to the Lord, but rather stuffed deep inside and covered over. This is a part of the superficial type of healing that Jeremiah 6:14 speaks about. The truth is that there is still a deep wound that has never been healed but has only been covered over as an oyster covers a grain of sand. The prophet Isaiah describes this situation:

> *"From the sole of the foot even to the head there is nothing sound in it, only bruises, welts, and raw wounds, not pressed out or bandaged, nor softened with oil."*
> Isaiah 1:6

Imagine that you suffered a physical laceration of your arm. Instead of cleaning it out, antisepticizing the wound, and sewing it up, you simply left it open, let all kinds of dirt get into it, and never tended to it at all. After a period of time, the wound would scab over and might even look as if it were healed, but underneath the outer layer would be a reservoir of infectious puss. In such a situation, each time pressure is put on the wound, more infectious puss is released into the body. Eventually, for true healing to come, someone must lance the wound, irrigate out all the infectious puss, cleanse and antisepticize the wound, and close it back up.

This is the type of picture that Isaiah is giving us regarding the inner man. A spiritual cleansing must occur, and when it does not, a person can walk around all his/her life with deep emotional or spiritual wounds that are severely infected but have never been "pressed out or bandaged, nor softened with oil."

Such was the case with Joe. Finally, he agreed to share the childhood experience that had come to his mind during prayer. However, he continued to maintain that the experience was not relevant; it was so insignificant that he hadn't even remembered it until that moment; besides, it didn't hurt any more; and he had forgiven his dad years ago.

Joe began to share by saying that when he was eight years old, one Friday night he had an opportunity to have two of his friends spend the night with him at his home. He was very excited about this and had been looking forward to the event for some time. Finally the day arrived. That evening the three boys were allowed to stay up later than normal, eat popcorn, and watch scary movies. They were having the time of their lives and finally fell asleep at about 1:00 A.M. When Joe awoke in the morning, much to his horror, he discovered that a terrible tragedy had occurred during the night. He had wet his bed. He desperately did not want his two friends to find out about the accident, so he quickly stripped the bed and hid the sheets and blankets.

However, Joe's mother found the bedding and discovered what had happened. She promptly let Joe's father know. He decided that an appropriate time to discipline Joe would be at the breakfast table in front of his friends and the rest of the family. Joe's father first exposed what had happened and then began to ridicule and shame Joe in front of the others. He called him a "bed wetter" and told him that they would have to buy him a big diaper to wear. Joe's dad let him know what a big disappointment it was for him to have an eight-year-old son who still wet the bed. After much derision and ridicule, Joe's father pulled down Joe's pants, bent him over his knee, and gave him a lengthy, bare-bottom spanking right there at the breakfast table in front of his friends.

Joe went on to share that after such total humiliation, he just wanted to sink through the floor and disappear. He also said that at that moment he wished he could have killed his dad, and that if he had a means to do so, he probably would have.

"But it doesn't bother me any more, and I haven't even remembered that experience for over thirty years," he added.

Realizing that there probably was some unresolved, emotional wounding bottled up inside, as though under a cork, I asked Joe if he would speak out in prayer to Jesus how he felt while his father was ridiculing and humiliating him in front of his friends at the table that morning many years ago. He agreed to do so. We bowed our heads and closed our eyes to pray, and I waited about ninety seconds for Joe to begin speaking to the Lord in prayer. But he was not saying anything. I thought that perhaps he had not understood that he was to pray out loud, so I finally invited again saying, "Go ahead and just speak out to the Lord how you felt that morning."

Suddenly this normally reserved, unemotional man burst into tears, and thirty years of stored up hurt, resentment, and anger came flowing out during the next 15 minutes. He wept and wept and wept as the covered over wound was finally lanced. I was then able to show Joe how Satan had used his own father unwittingly to communicate to Joe as a small boy his message of identity and destiny. Satan's message was: "You are nothing but a bed wetter. There is just something inherently wrong with you. No matter how hard you try, you will never succeed at anything in life. You are a shame to your family and an embarrassment to God."

Joe later admitted that this really was how he had felt deep inside all his adult life. He had always believed that the deck was stacked against him, and that no matter what he did, circumstances beyond his control always caused him to fail, through no fault of his own. This would create great frustration and anger which, when acted upon, would further embarrass and shame him.

After releasing all that infectious, emotional puss from the inner wound, Joe was then able to forgive his father from his heart and afterwards go to God, his heavenly Father, and ask Him to reveal the truth of who Joe really was and why he was here. All Joe's life the Lord had been wanting to impart to Joe His message of identity and destiny, but the devil's message was already so strongly established deep inside. Up until now he could never before receive God's opinion of him. As a result, even though Joe was nearly forty years old, on the inside, in the emotional realm, there had always been living a fearful, insecure, eight-year-old boy.

Finally that day as the cork was popped, all the hurt and anger of the humiliated, eight-year-old boy inside were released, and for the first time Joe was able to allow himself to receive God's message of identity and destiny and to be the man God created him to be without feeling inside like a bed wetter. Joe's entire life was changed that day. He later reported that it was like having lived his whole life in black and white up until that point and then discovering a whole new world of color.

It is easy to see how Joe's father was used unintentionally as a pawn of Satan to impart to Joe the devil's message of identity and destiny. He had no idea of the impact that experience would have on Joe's life for years to come. Joe's father was simply attempting to discipline his son, but he had no understanding of blessing and cursing or of God's "ancient ways." Consequently, he delivered a message resulting in an inner image in Joe's mind that caused Joe to spend many years trying to hack his way through the jungle with a machete instead of riding in a Mercedes on the highway to get to the goal. The Bible tells us that *"for lack of knowledge My people perish."* (Hosea 4:6)

FALSE PLUMB LINES

When identity and destiny messages are sent to us at critical times in life, they establish on the inside of us images of ourselves, God, and others. When these messages come from Satan rather than from God, images established are not in accordance with truth, but rather are false images. As adults, we usually interpret our circumstances each day in accordance with the images established inside our hearts. As a result, often times the way we perceive circumstances and events taking place in our lives is not in line with God's truth but rather is in accordance with false images. These images were established in our hearts through wrong identity and destiny messages. Amos gives us a word picture of this.

> *"Thus He showed me, and behold, the Lord was standing by a vertical wall, with a plumb line in His hand. And the Lord said to me, `What do you see, Amos?' And I said, `A plumb line.' Then the Lord said, `Behold I am about to put a plumb line in the midst of My people Israel. I will spare them no longer."* Amos 7:7-8

First, in order to understand this verse, we must ask these questions, "What is a plumb line?" and "What is it used for?" A plumb line is a metal weight on the end of a string which is used to determine if a wall under construction is vertical or not. A plumb line always hangs vertically. If one were to try to build a brick wall without the aid of a plumb line, the wall would probably deviate off the vertical to some extent and thus have insufficient structural integrity. However, something worse than using no plumb line at all is to use a perverted plumb line - one which you believe hangs straight, but in actuality is hanging crooked. This is the situation into which the above Scripture passage from Amos is speaking.

One time I conducted a word study of the word "wall" in the Old Testament, and I discovered that it is very often describing the human heart. In the above passage, God is speaking through the prophet Amos about the condition of the corporate heart of His people, Israel. He is saying that they have constructed the walls of their society using a plumb line that is not straight but rather is perverted. God is now coming to hang a straight plumb line (His Word) along side of their seemingly vertical wall in order to show them how crooked their wall really is.

Suppose when you are a very small child, you are going to begin building the wall of your heart through answering the question, "Who am I?" You hang out a plumb line to determine the answer to this question so as to be able to place the first brick in your wall. However, an enemy who hates you comes near where you hang out your plumb line and hides in the bushes with a powerful magnet in his hand. The magnet draws the plumb line off center, but you don't know it. When you look at the plumb line, you believe that it is straight and begin building your wall accordingly. All the enemy needs to do is leave the magnet in the bushes near you in order to wreak destruction in your life. This is a good scheme that runs itself.

The magnet in this example is the devil's message of identity and destiny. Once these become established images of truth in the heart, the entire life, thought patterns, emotional response patterns, etc. are constructed using these false plumb lines as a basis. God is wanting to expose these false, plumb-line images and to reestablish His message of truth regarding your identity and destiny.

I believe that Satan really has a three-fold plan in mind. This plan is: 1) to distort the image of who God has created you to be, 2) to drive you out of the place in which God has called you to dwell, and 3) to steal your inheritance. I have observed that this occurs over and over again within people regarding their family, careers, jobs, and churches. This is exactly what was happening in Joe's life, as I described earlier. Because of a distorted image of himself, of God, and how life worked in general, Joe's anger was about to cost him his job and family. The purpose of the enemy was to steal that inheritance which God was attempting to give to him.

BATTERY CABLE CORROSION

I meet many people who feel as though they have been crying out to God for help and answers in their lives, but He never seems to pay much attention to them, and nothing ever changes. Although that appears to be the situation, we know that God is not really the problem. God is like a battery, continually sending out power and life. The devil cannot stop the power of God from flowing, so he does the next best thing. He corrodes the battery-cable connection. You and I are like battery cables. If you have ever looked under the hood of your car, you have probably noticed that there is a little metal ring at the end of the battery cable which must fit down over the end of the battery terminal. If the inside of this cable ring becomes coated with corrosion, it doesn't matter how much power is stored within the battery; none of it will be able to get to the cable to flow to the starter mechanism. When this is the case, you can sit in your car and continue to turn the ignition key in frustration, but no power can reach the starter. Your conclusion may be that the battery is dead.

God loves you and is continually wanting to send to you His love, life, power, and help. However, if the enemy has been able to establish his message of identity and destiny within you, then the resulting internal images serve to insulate you from God's life and love, just as corrosion on a battery cable ring isolates the starter from the battery power. God is not withholding His love and help from you. He is wanting to expose to you the corrosion that would keep you from experiencing His love and help in your life.

We have seen that the entire course of a person's adult life can be determined through the impartation of either God's or Satan's messages of identity and destiny during the childhood years. The primary agents of this impartation are parents and other significant adults. Let us now turn our attention to the primary vehicles that deliver these identity and destiny messages: **BLESSING** and **CURSING**.

Chapter 3
BLESSING AND CURSING

*"Now the Lord said to Abram, `Go forth from your country, and from your relatives and from your father's house, to the land which I will show you; and I will make you a great nation, and I will bless you, and make your name great; and so you shall be a blessing; and I will bless those who bless you, and the one who curses you I will curse, and **in you all the families of the earth shall be blessed.**'"* Genesis 12:1-3.

This was a covenant promise which God made to Abraham foretelling the coming and the purpose of Jesus Christ. Since this statement was made by God, He has been in the business of blessing families. God's purpose in Jesus' coming was to bless all the families of the earth. The primary unit through which God has committed Himself to work is the family. God is the "blesser." The devil is the "curser." Through Jesus Christ, God is intent on blessing all the families of the earth.

Blessing is God's primary mechanism of imparting His message of identity and destiny into your life. Therefore, it is important to understand the meaning of the word "blessing." Gary Smalley and John Trent have written an excellent book entirely dedicated to expounding on the biblical meaning of the concept of blessing. Their book simply entitled "The Blessing" will give you tremendous, further insight into the meaning of blessing.[1]

Smalley and Trent define the blessing that should

come to us through parents as containing the following five key elements:

"The family blessing" includes:

- MEANINGFUL TOUCH
- A SPOKEN MESSAGE
- ATTATCHING HIGH VALUE TO THE
    ONE BEING BLESSED
- PICTURING A SPECIAL FUTURE FOR
    THE ONE BEING BLESSED
- AN ACTIVE COMMITMENT TO FULFILL
    THE BLESSING [2]

BLESSING: TO EMPOWER TO PROSPER

For our purpose here, a simple definition of **BLESSING** is: to receive, accept, ascribe high value to, and consider a person as a success. In the Hebrew language, the verb to bless is "**BARUCH**." One of the primary meanings of this word is, "**TO EMPOWER TO PROSPER**." A good definition, then, of cursing would be "**TO DISEMPOWER FROM PROSPERING**." What does it mean to prosper? In our North American culture, we primarily think of prosperity in terms of money. However, economic prosperity is not all that this word entails. We could better define this verb "to prosper" as to thrive, succeed, or do well. In the Hebrew language, this word primarily means "**TO HAVE A PLEASANT FULFILLING JOURNEY**." Thus, to prosper would mean to have a pleasant journey through your life.

So, in combining these definitions, to bless, (**BARUCH**), would mean to empower the one being blessed to thrive, succeed, do well, and to have a pleasant, fulfilling journey through life. On the other hand, to curse would mean to dis-empower or to disable the one being cursed from thriving, succeeding, or having a pleasant or fulfilling journey through life.

BLUE WATER (BLESSING) OR HYDROCHLORIC ACID (CURSING)

One of the best pictures of this came to me one day as I watched my wife, Jan, watering her house plants. Jan is an expert at growing house plants. As she cares for them, they thrive and grow exceedingly large and healthy. When people come to visit, they frequently comment on Jan's marvelous ability to grow house plants.

When it is time to water the plants, Jan mixes a blue powder containing plant nutrient of some sort with water and pours just the right amount on each plant. I noticed that after each application of this "blue water," the plants seem to perk up and really be full of life. Suppose, however, that one day Jan decided to pour hydrochloric acid on her plants instead of the nutrient-laden water. How might they respond? Instead of thriving, opening up their pores and craving more, the plants would close all their little pores, and attempt to repel as much of the acid as possible.

This example above is a good picture of the power of blessing and cursing. Parents with their words, attitudes, and actions possess the ability to bless or curse the identities of their children. Blessing is like pouring nutrient-laden, blue water over the child's inner being, while cursing is like pouring hydrochloric acid over the inner being. One empowers the child to prosper, while the other cripples and disables. Blessing imparts God's message of identity and destiny, while cursing imparts Satan's message of the same.

JOSHUA AND THE HAMBURGER

Many times we inadvertently curse the identity of those who are closest to us without even realizing it. The Lord made this very real to me one day as I sat in a restaurant with my family, attempting to get my four-year-old son to eat his hamburger. Joshua and I had come to an irreconcilable stand-off regarding the hamburger. We had gone to the restaurant after church on a Sunday, and he had wanted a hamburger for lunch. However, when the meal came, I noticed that the hamburger was much too big for Joshua to eat without its being cut. So, I simply reached over with my knife and fork and cut his hamburger in half.

I then said, "There, now it will be much easier for you to eat." Joshua looked at me with an anguished look of shock and disbelief. With tears starting to roll out of his eyes, he said, "You ruined it! I'm not going to eat it. Fix it, Daddy."

"I can't fix it, Josh," I replied. "What do you want me to do? Get some super glue and glue it back together?" I tried for several minutes to convince him that the hamburger would taste just the same whether it was cut or not. However, he still refused and demanded that I put it back together or at least get him a new hamburger.

Since neither bribery nor threats seemed to motivate Joshua to stop crying and eat, it suddenly dawned on me to pray and ask the Lord how to solve the problem.

"Lord," I prayed, "I'm engaged in a power struggle with a four-year-old, and I'm losing. How can I get Josh to eat his hamburger?" The Lord quickly spoke right back into my spirit that I should repent and ask my son's forgiveness. I thought to myself, "Why should I repent? I'm right. I can't repent, if I'm the one who's right. He should eat his hamburger, and I was right to cut it, because it was too big for him to handle."

Then the Holy Spirit reminded me of a well-known scripture when Jesus told his disciples,

> *"Do you not yet see or understand?
> Do you have a hardened heart? Having
> eyes, do you not see? And having ears, do
> you not hear?"*   Mark 8:17-18

The Lord then spoke to me saying, "You are just like these disciples. You have physical eyes and ears, but you are not understanding the real issues in this matter. You think that you are talking about a hamburger, but that is not the issue. When your son said to you, 'You ruined it,' he was not talking about the hamburger. He was talking about his value to you as your son. His identity was cursed by you, and his value as a person, in general, and as your son, in specific, is what was ruined, not the hamburger. However, you have had no eyes to see or ears to hear the real issue."

"The hamburger is not really the issue of concern at

31

all, but the message conveyed to your son through your method and attitude is of great concern." I was beginning to see something, so I asked the Lord for more clarification. The Holy Spirit continued speaking into my spirit, "When you reached over and cut the food on Joshua's plate, you didn't extend to him the courtesy of communicating with him your intentions before just treating his plate as your own. Then when he reacted, you continued to treat him as if he were the one with an attitude problem and didn't acknowledge his feelings on the matter at all. You treated him as if he had no feelings or as if his feelings didn't matter. How would you like it if someone uninvited reached over to your plate and began to tinker with your food?"

"The message you sent to Joshua in acting without consulting him was, `You are not really of any value. Your opinion doesn't really count. You're just a child, and I'm an adult. I can treat you however I please, and I don't need to consider your opinion or feelings. You have no right to make decisions, because you have no wisdom and are of no value.'"

"Then as you persisted in your position that you are right and your son needs to stop the commotion and eat, you have sent him the message that you don't care about him at all and that the issue (the hamburger) is really more important to you than he is as a person. Through all this, you have sent to your son a message that you are arbitrary, uncaring and authoritarian. Furthermore, your message continues that in your sight he is worthless, not worthy even of taking charge over his own plate of food, incapable of making any decision, and nothing but a bother to you."

I finally saw that although I had been right on the external issue, I had conveyed to my little son a devastating and destructive message through my blindness to his feelings and my focus on the external issue. All that time I had thought that we were talking about a hamburger, while, in actuality, we were discussing Joshua's value as a person. I had severely cursed his identity and had no idea that I had done so. It was as though I had poured hydrochloric acid upon my own son and thought that I was right in doing so.

The Lord spoke all this to me in just a few quick seconds. I decided to check it out by asking Joshua if this were true. So I asked, "Joshua, have I made you feel as though you're not very important to me?" His countenance suddenly changed, and he began to look at me as if maybe somehow I really did understand.

He answered, "Yes."

I continued, "Did you feel that Daddy got in your space without asking first?"

"Yes," he exclaimed.

I then said, "Joshua, I'm sorry. I can now see that I was very wrong to treat you that way. I should have talked to you before I cut your food. Will you forgive me?"

He replied, "Yes, Daddy."

I continued, "I made you feel that eating the hamburger was more important to me than you are. That is not at all true. I love you very much, and you are much more important to me than the issue of whether you eat this hamburger or not. I was wrong to talk to you that way. Will you forgive me?"

"Yes, Daddy," he responded. I then offered to buy

Josh a new hamburger since I had, in fact, violated his personal identity and removed his choice regarding the first one. However, now that the identity problem was solved, he thought that the hamburger on his plate would be just fine, and it really was much easier to eat cut in half. As soon as the problem regarding his value as a person was solved, the problem with the hamburger vanished.

FOR LACK OF KNOWLEDGE, MY PEOPLE PERISH

Many times when parents are attempting to motivate their children or stimulate them to excellence, without realizing it they are actually communicating a message to the son or daughter that no matter what level of achievement or acccomplishment he or she might attain, the child is still not a success in the sight of the parents. There is something God-given on the inside of every one of us that longs to hear the words **"Son (or Honey), I'm proud of you,"** from our dad and mom. This is a form of blessing which God intended to flow frequently through parents to their children. However, because of the lack of such from their own parents, many parents have never learned to allow their children to succeed in their sight and to express such to them. This was the case with Sandy and her father.

Sandy's father grew up in a rural area in one of the southern states during the time of the Great Depression. He had never had an opportunity to gain a good education for himself since he was forced to drop out of high school to go to work to help support the family. As a result, Sandy's father had vowed that all of his children would go to college. He had hopes that they would continue their studies in medical or other professional fields.

Sandy knew that academic performance was very important to her dad, so she took her schoolwork very seriously. Fortunately, Sandy was also highly gifted academically. Her grades were usually top-notch. During the first semester of her sophomore year in high school, Sandy took some unusually difficult college level classes. The academic load was quite a challenge to her, but she managed to come home with a report card showing "A's" in all classes, except one with a "B."

Proudly Sandy presented her report card to her father expecting to hear words of praise and affirmation from him. After carefully perusing the document, he looked up and chided his startled daughter. "How come you got only a "B" in this class?" he challenged. "You've been spending too much time in sports activities. You need to work harder. Let's see if you can pull that grade up next semester. If you want to make something out of your life, you're going to have to get good grades!"

Sandy's heart was devastated. It felt as if her father had plunged a knife into her heart and was twisting it, gouging and tearing her heart to shreds. She had tried so hard to please her father, and yet it wasn't enough. That night as Sandy lay awake in her bed with an inner wound that wouldn't stop bleeding, she vowed that the next semester she would get "straight A's" in all classes, even though she was still taking college-level, honor classes.

Sure enough at the end of the second semester, Sandy came home with "straight A's" in every class on her report card. This time her father would have to acknowledge her, tell her that she was a success, and say that he was proud of her. Confidently, she handed her report card to her father when he arrived home from work that evening. Again, he thoroughly surveyed the report and then looked up into his daughter's hopeful eyes and remarked, "Obviously the classes you took were too easy if you can just breeze through them like that and get all "A's.""

Little did her father realize the night his daughter came to him with her report card, that he held a key in his hand with which he could open or close the door to Sandy's future success. He could use the key of blessing to empower her to prosper, or he could refuse to use that key and, by default, through ignorance, use the key of cursing to pour hydrochloric acid, so to speak, on her inner being, thus crippling and disabling her.

Since her father failed to use the blessing key that night, Sandy's grades soon deteriorated to "D's" and "F's." In her junior year of high school she became pregnant, moved in with her boyfriend, and dropped out of school all together. All her father's dreams for her life were shattered. He said he wanted nothing more to do with her. It wasn't until years later when Sandy gave her life to Jesus Christ that her relationship with her father began to be reconciled, and healing and restoration began to come to her life.

Blessing is meant to impart God's image of identity and destiny into your life. When Satan's image of identity and destiny is delivered, a three-fold scheme almost always is set in motion, as it was in Sandy's life. This was mentioned earlier, but it's worthy of repeating at this point. Through the cursing of identity, Satan hopes to:

1. Distort or replace entirely your image of who God has called you to be.

2. Drive you out of your place of habitation, the place of protection and residence which is yours. (Your family, marriage, church, employment, home, city, country.)

3. Steal your inheritance –that which God has meant to be an inheritance or heritage to you. (Your children, finances, ministry, pension, relationships.)

THE ROLE OF PARENTS

Whether they realize it or not, parents hold a powerful key to the future lives of their children in blessing and cursing. Through one, parents can literally empower their children to prosper and thrive as adults in their marriages, family relationships, businesses, ministries, health, and finances. Through the other, parents can mar, cripple, and literally prevent their children from thriving and prospering in all these same areas of adult life. This is again due to the fact that blessing is God's ordained method of imparting identity and destiny to people, and parents are God's ordained agents through whom this is to come. Unfortunately, many of our parents failed to have knowledge of their job description before they became parents. As a result, many of us received the devil's message, by default, throughout most of our growing- up years.

As I studied the ancient Hebrew culture in the Bible, I discovered that there are seven essential times when God intended to impart a powerful message of identity and destiny into the life of each person. In Bible times, no one had to have any knowledge of the need to bless and give out God's message at these appointed times. God had strategically placed right within the culture ceremonies, customs, habits, and other mechanisms to ensure that lives were permeated with His message of identity and destiny. Parents could not do it wrong. All they had to do was just follow what everybody in that culture did, and it would come out right.

However, in modern day North America, over the last 150 years or so, the devil has systematically ripped out of our American culture every ceremony, custom, habit, and other protective mechanisms that God had established to ensure our being blessed. As a result, if parents today just adhere to our present culture, by default, they will miss imparting God's message of identity and destiny into their children's lives according to God's plan. In my understanding of blessing at these seven special times of life, I can't see that the culture of Christian people in the church today is really very different from that of those outside the church. Many Christians believe that if they pray for their children, take them to church, put them in a Christian school, teach them the Bible, make sure that they have Christian friends, love them, and properly discipline them, they should grow up to be godly Christian adults. Although all these activities are good, none of them actually delivers God's message of identity and destiny when most needed. As a result, I have run into many broken-hearted parents who are weeping over the devastation that has occurred in the lives of their teen-age and adult children.

"For lack of knowledge My people perish."
Hosea 4:6

The good news is that Jesus Christ has come to this earth as a Redeemer to restore to your life and to the lives of your children everything that the kingdom of darkness has stolen. Through a 3-day seminar we conduct entitled **FAMILY FOUNDATIONS ANCIENT PATHS SEMINAR**, we have seen over and over again the Father God impart into peoples' lives His blessing in every area where they failed to receive blessing through the default or active cursing by parents. We have also seen the entire lives of young adults changed as their parents received understanding of the seven crucial times of blessing, have asked their children's forgiveness, and have then blessed the children. (For more information on how you can participate in an **ANCIENT PATHS SEMINAR** in your area see page 108 in the back of this book.)

CURSING BINDS; BLESSING LOOSES

In working with married couples, I first began to discover that there were many situations and conflicts that could not be solved horizontally just between the husband and wife. Many of the issues stemmed back to unhealthy ties to one or both parents. Genesis 2:24 states: *"For this cause a man shall leave his father and mother, and shall cleave to his wife; and they shall become one flesh."*

I noticed that many couples had many areas where they were not cleaving together. So I began to ask the Lord why this was. The answer came very clearly from the above scripture. In any area of your life where you don't leave, you cannot cleave.

What does the Bible mean "to leave father and mother?" I don't believe that this is talking about a geographic change of location necessarily. It is more likely speaking of an emotional leaving or a leaving in the heart. You don't have to move to another city when you marry in order to leave your father and mother. But the Lord began to show me that if in any area of a man's life, he has not left his father and mother, he **CANNOT** cleave to his wife. So it is vital that when a couple marries, there is a healthy, emotional leaving of the father and mother.

The next obvious question that I began to ask was, "What causes a man or woman to leave or not leave, since he or she can't cleave where he or she didn't leave?" I began to find a pattern as I studied lineages of people in the Bible, as well as observing the lives of people to whom I was ministering. Those who were blessed by their parents were able to leave in a healthy way, and those who were not blessed did not properly leave. I found that in the areas of a person's life in which he or she was blessed, that person could leave, and thus when married, cleave. On the other hand, in the areas in which he or she was not blessed, the cleaving could not take place after marriage. Blessing of parents looses the identity to leave and thus to cleave. Cursing (or by default lack of blessing) binds the identity to the parent and hinders cleaving.

There are two primary reactions to cursing of identity, either of which equally binds one to the parent and hinders cleaving in a marriage:

1. Decision to isolate from the parent and write him out of one's life. "If he won't bless me, I don't need

his blessing or acceptance. I don't care what he thinks. It doesn't matter." In attempting to cut the parent out of your life, you actually bind yourself to him. You also loose an internal, emotional focus which will often reproduce in your own life, or sometimes in the life of your marriage partner, the very qualities you hate in your parent.

2. Decision to continue striving after the blessing of the parent no matter how long it takes or what it costs. "If I can just make enough money, or do something very important, or win enough people to Christ, then he will have to acknowledge me and bless me." In striving after the parent's blessing, you bind yourself to the parent and are not free to cleave to a spouse.

FREEDOM FOR JIM

Jim was a man who had made the #1 decision above regarding his mother and had reproduced in his wife the very qualities that he had hated in his mother. Jim's wife first came to me for help, stating that she loved Jim very deeply, but there were certain situations in their marriage that made life intolerable for her. She was considering leaving her husband. She went on to describe that Jim simply refused to take any type of responsibility at home. He acknowledged that many duties were indeed his responsibility, but then he failed to follow through with any action.

Jim's wife explained that the bank was about to repossess their house, because they had not made any payments for several months. They actually had sufficient money, but Jim just "never got around" to making the mortgage payment. He acknowledged that it was his job to pay the bills, keep the yard, maintain the cars, and shovel the walks in the winter. However, he never really did any of these things. Consequently, Jim's wife had begrudgingly taken over all of these duties and was extremely weary and frustrated.

The following week I met Jim. Initially, I asked him how his marriage was going. He replied, "Oh, we have our ups and downs like everyone else, but we really love each other and have a good stable marriage. I can't really complain about anything." I noticed that there was quite a disparity between his perception and his wife's perception of their marriage.

As I began to confront Jim regarding his irresponsibility, as his wife had reported, he acknowledged that these were his duties, but he just seemed to forget or "space them out" all the time. At first I began to work with Jim on time management and goal setting, but try as I might, he never fulfilled his responsibilities around the house. I began to understand his wife's frustration.

We began to pray together to ask the Lord to reveal the root of his problem. One day I began to ask Jim a series of questions regarding his mother, and the answers began to come. Jim was the second born of two children. His mother overtly favored his older sister and conveyed a message to him that he couldn't do much of anything right.

Jim's mother wanted to spare him the embarrassment of making any mistakes, so she constantly followed up everything that he did and redid it so that it would be "right." When she asked Jim to set the table, it was never to her satisfaction, so she always came and reset it after him. She also instilled in him that making a mistake was a terrible thing, and he should always avoid mistakes at all costs. Every time Jim's mom would redo one of his tasks and criticize him for the job he had done, it deeply wounded the heart of the little boy. It was a form of cursing his identity and was very painful emotionally. Jim learned from a very early age that he couldn't do anything right to please his mother, so the best way to avoid being hurt and criticized, he thought, was not doing anything at all for her. He was then scolded for not doing the task, but that was far less painful than being chastised for doing it "wrong." Besides, his mom would then come and do it the way she wanted, anyway, and he was off the hook altogether.

When Jim married, what kind of woman do you think he looked for? You are right: one exactly the opposite of his mother. He found a wonderful, Christian girl, who loved Jim just the way he was and never criticized him or told him he did it wrong, as his mom used to do. However, because Jim had never been blessed by his mom and had never forgiven her in his heart for all the cursing and criticism, deep inside he was still tied to her. He carried an emotional expectation that "eventually women will criticize you and curse your identity," even though his wife had never yet treated him that way. It was this unhealthy tie to his mother that was wreaking havoc in Jim's marriage. Over the years, Jim had forced his wife into the same role his mother had played.

It was the unconscious fear of being criticized that

caused Jim to default on all his domestic responsibilities. He left his wife with only three bad options: 1. Do nothing and watch everything go down the tubes. 2. Continue to nag Jim and try to get him to perform, usually with little success and great frustration. 3. Give up and do it herself. She had eventually chosen the third option, much to Jim's relief. Now he thought everything was great, but she was frustrated beyond belief. The net result was that Jim had forced his wife into the role of being his mother rather than his wife and had reproduced in her the same criticism and cursing of his identity that he had so hated in his mother.

Without realizing it, Jim was still bound to his mother and was not free to cleave to his wife and be a proper husband to her. Until he was able to truly forgive his mom from his heart for the constant cursing of his identity and then go to the Lord and receive from Him the blessing of his correct identity and destiny, he would not be liberated.

Tremendous freedom and healing have come to many couples just like Jim and his wife as we have ministered to them in seminars. They have discovered that their marital difficulties are not merely horizontal. Often one or both marriage partners are still tied to a parent through cursing of identity and are virtually unable to properly cleave.

God intended for each person to be blessed by his or her parents at many times in life, thereby imparting His image of identity and destiny. However, there really are seven special times which I will mention later. Blessing is such a powerful, releasing force that the Bible does not record any miracles, preaching, or ministry whatsoever of Jesus Christ until He received the audible blessing of His Father on His life at the Jordan River.

> *"Now it came about when all the people were baptized, that Jesus also was baptized, and while He was praying, heaven was opened, and the Holy Spirit descended upon Him in bodily form as a dove, and a voice came out of heaven, `Thou art My beloved Son, in Thee I am well pleased.'"*
> Luke 3:21-22

I have come to call blessing "Generational Evangelism." Blessing your children at key times in life imparts to them God's message of who they are and where they are going. It also virtually ensures that that image will be lived out in adulthood and probably carried on naturally to the next generation, your grandchildren. With this in mind, let us now turn our attention to consider God's wisdom in placing protective measures in cultures and societies of the world so that people would naturally be blessed and not cursed.

---

[1] Gary Smalley and John Trent, Phd., The Blessing, (Nashville, Thomas Nelson Publishers, 1986)
[2]   IBID., P.24

Chapter 4
GOD'S BLESSING THROUGH CULTURAL TRADITIONS

Blessing is, indeed, the key to the establishment of God's image of identity and destiny on the inside of people. As I mentioned in the last chapter, when I began to study the concept of blessing in the Bible, I found that there are seven special times in life when blessing needs to be given. I think that it was so important to God that His message of identity and destiny be taught at these times that He placed in the ancient Jewish culture ceremonies, customs, laws, and other protective measures to ensure that people would get His message rather than Satan's.

I next was drawn to look at other cultures of the world and was astounded to discover that every culture I examined had similar protective mechanisms at key times in life. I found the same types of ceremonies, customs, and laws in the Polynesian culture, the South American Indian culture, the African tribal culture, the North American Indian culture, and many other cultures of the world. Only our modern day, American culture is the exception. These ways of ensuring that blessing occurred in the lives of people growing up did not just independently develop out of nowhere, but rather, it became obvious to me that God originally saw to it that every culture was infused with His ancient ways.

Even in our North American culture, as recently as 150 years ago, every child growing up had a **FATHER**, a **FAMILY**, and a **FUTURE**. People knew who they were and where they were going. Not so any more. All the time I meet people who are 30, 40 and 50 years old who are trying to figure out what they want to do "when they grow up." Over the last few generations, Satan has systematically stripped our culture of every one of the protective measures that God originally placed there. Devoid of God's identity and destiny message, we now have at least two entire generations of people without identity or destiny.

> *"Where there is no vision, the people perish."* (Proverbs 29:18)

The greatest tragedy on earth is not death but life without purpose. The Bible tells us that God planned for you before the foundation of the earth. (Ephesians 1:3-6) I believe that He intended, through your parents, to infuse powerfully in you purpose and vision for your life. The fact that you were born is evidence that God has a plan for you. A Boeing 747 never just rolled out of the hangar with no purpose, vision, or plan for its usage. Not one piece of aluminum was shaped to build such an aircraft until the purpose was thoroughly thought through, a complete plan drawn on paper, and a detailed engineering study completed. Physical manufacturing of a product is begun only after the entire project is completed, from vision to end result on paper. If men are smart enough to operate in this fashion, how much more so is God? (Isaiah 46:9-10) Your very life is evidence enough that your purpose for being is already complete in the mind of God. No one is an accident on this earth. However, many people in our society feel as though they are and spend a lifetime attempting to discover and plug into their purpose. This is a result of our allowing the kingdom of darkness to remove God's cultural safeguards and ancient ways.

*"But the people who do know their God
shall be strong and do exploits."*
(Daniel 11:32)

When people have been given an internal image and vision of who they are and where they are going, then they can stretch themselves to do the exploits of God. However, when this has not been done, people are overrun and consumed by daily problems of life and maintenance functions. God never intended for people to expend so much emotional energy in just everyday living, nor did He plan for life to be as complicated as it has become today. Unfortunately, God's ancient ways are no longer intact in our society, and most of us now live as people in a threatened city without protective walls.

A CITY WITHOUT WALLS

In ancient times, when a significant population settled in one place, and there began to be commerce and accumulation of economic substance, the settlement became ripe for pillage and plundering by neighboring, enemy peoples. As a result, one of the first things that was done when a city sprang up was to build a tall, thick wall around it. The purpose of the wall was to keep out enemies. As soon as the wall was in place, the city was secure. Only a relatively small number of warriors needed to stand guard on the wall and repel any sort of marauding enemy. Before the wall was in place, however, every man had to be a warrior. Much of his time and energy was consumed with concern about enemy activity.

Once a good wall was built, very few enemies were even seen any more. It was much easier to attack a settlement without walls completed than a walled one. After a couple of generations had lived within a walled city, so few enemies ever appeared that many inhabitants had very little awareness of the purpose of the walls. The problem with walls is that just as effectively as they keep enemies out, they also keep inhabitants in. This can oftentimes be inconvenient and unproductive.

FISHING AND CITY WALLS

Suppose a fisherman, dwelling in a walled city, quite by accident discovers that the largest fish can be caught in a nearby pool outside the city walls only in the middle of the night. However, the gates to the city close at dusk. Since this man lives adjacent to the city wall, he decides to dig a small hole through the city wall through which he can come and go at night. He does not believe that the city is really harmed by his small breach in the wall.

However, one evening one of his friends inquires as to how he is able to catch such large fish. He shares the secret with his friend, who then also digs a small hole through the wall near his own house. You know the scenario from there. Soon everyone who lives along the wall has a small breach in the wall through which he can personally come and go at his own discretion. If we follow this through for a couple of generations, all we have left are a few pillars standing where the wall used to be. However, it is very convenient for all the inhabitants to come and go as they please. News of this situation soon reaches enemies who then begin to raid and plunder the city again.

Now under this circumstance, every male citizen is again a warrior. No longer can children play outside alone. Every minor task becomes a life-threatening experience. It is now dangerous to go down the street to buy a loaf of bread, or even go outside to the outhouse at night because of the danger of enemy snipers. The lives of these inhabitants are now consumed with concern for the security of their families and households rather than concern for the pursuit of their calling and life purpose. This is a physical picture of the spiritual status of our present society. Many of us are so absorbed with the daily maintenance tasks of living in a city without walls that we have no time or energy to pursue or even discover the purpose and calling of our lives.

Suppose, then, that the city council in those ancient times decides to rebuild the city walls. Now the grandchildren of the first fisherman who punched the initial hole through the wall own an entire fishing business employing 100 people who all depend upon fishing at night. When the city council announces that the new wall will extend right across their fishing path, all 100 of these families are up in arms about the idea. The problem with rebuilding walls is that it always costs very dearly for the generation in which the walls are rebuilt. They are forced to make a choice either for their own short-term, personal benefit or for the benefit of the entire city and future generations.

*"And they that shall be of thee shall build the old
waste places: thou shalt raise up the foundations*

of many generations; and thou shalt be called,
`The repairer of the breach, the restorer of paths
to dwell in.'"   (Isaiah 58:12)KJV

I believe that God is calling us in this generation to be the people who will rebuild the walls that have been made into ruins. We are called to repair the breaches in the walls and to restore the ancient paths of God. The ceremonies, practices, and habits, infused by God into culture as natural and customary experiences, impart identity and destiny to children at those seven special times of life. These are like walls around a vulnerable city. We have so let these walls deteriorate that when we begin to talk about restoring the **ANCIENT PATHS**, most of us have to ask, "What ancient paths?" This is why the Lord exhorts us to:

"Stand by the ways and SEE and ASK for the
ancient paths, where the good way is and walk in
it; and you shall find rest for your souls."
    (Jeremiah 6:16)

As I have mentioned, the Lord showed me seven very vulnerable times in life when we will receive either God's image of who we are and where we are going or Satan's image. The protective walls to ensure that we get God's message and not the devil's are those ceremonies, habits, customs and laws declared by God to His people. When the walls are not in place, then most of the time, by default, we receive the wrong message, which results in rejection, wounding, and cursing of identity.

WHAT'S IN A NAME?

When blessing does take place at those crucial times, it releases an extraordinary, inner security and confidence. One important way of blessing children in the ancient Hebrew culture was through the given name. In that culture, a person's name was very important. It was given by the parents after carefully seeking the Lord and it usually contained worthy character qualities and often even a job description. The name was announced in a ceremony and celebration which honored the child on the 8th day after birth. Since the job description was often in the name which the parents had received from God, many people had knowledge of their calling and purpose in life right from the 8th day. They did not have to strive and struggle to do something important to create value in their adult life or spend several decades attempting to discover their life purpose.

Elijah is a good example of a man whose name contained a job description. Elijah came on the scene during the reign of King Ahab in Israel. Ahab had taken unto himself a foreign wife by the name of Jezebel from the land of Sidon (modern day Lebanon). Jezebel's people, the Sidonians, worshipped the idolatrous gods. During the reign of King Ahab over Israel, his wife, Jezebel, was single-handedly able to cause almost the entire nation of Israel to forsake God-Jehovah and worship Baal.

When Elijah was named on the 8th day after birth, he also received in his name his calling in life. Elijah means "**JEHOVAH IS GOD.**" His job as a prophet was to turn the nation from Baal worship back to serving the living God, Jehovah. Every time that Elijah's name was spoken, it was a declaration that Baal is not God, but Jehovah is God. Even when he was a little boy, and his parents would call, "Elijah," they were speaking forth his purpose: to declare that Jehovah is God.

"Come here, **JEHOVAH IS GOD**." "No, no, **JEHOVAH IS GOD**." Every time Elijah's name was spoken, his life's purpose was stated. As Elijah came into his adulthood, I'm sure that there was no question in his mind who he was and what his purpose was. That was an established image on the inside of him. It didn't matter what other kids called him at school or what anybody else thought. His purpose and calling in life had been imparted to him from God through his parents from the 8th day after birth and were unshakable within him.

Because of his confidence in God and the calling on his life, Elijah was able to challenge and defeat 450 prophets of Baal on Mount Carmel and turn the nation of Israel back to God. (I Kings 18) Elijah's name was, indeed, a great blessing to him.

On the other hand, there are many today whose parents arbitrarily choose for them a name without any sense of destiny or purpose. I remember hearing about a neighbor boy with whom I played as a child. When he became a father, he named his firstborn child after our dog. We had a friendly St. Bernard dog which used to visit this neighbor's home daily, because my friend's mom would feed him. Apparently, this neighbor boy really liked our dog's name and therefore used it for his firstborn daughter years later. There was nothing wrong with the dog's name, but what a heritage to give to his child! Can you imagine later on trying to explain to his child that he named her after a dog?

PARENTS ARE STRONGMEN

A family is a spiritual entity, not just a collection of people living under the same roof. There is a spiritual glue that unites a family, just as there is a "nuclear glue" that bonds the particles of an atom together. When an atom is split, it does not affect just that one atom. Instead, it initiates a chain reaction with far-reaching and oftentimes devastating consequences. The same is true of a family. There is a spiritual protection within the confines of a family, and if there is a break, there are far-reaching consequences in the family, too.

A family unit is created when a covenant is made between a man and a woman in marriage. I am absolutely convinced that something supernatural happens in the spirit realm at every legitimate wedding. A new spiritual unit is created where before there were only two individuals. The difference from a spiritual warfare perspective is the difference between defending yourself from on top of a pile of bricks or defending yourself from inside a brick fort. There is a spiritual protection in marriage as opposed to just living together. This is one of the ancient paths of God.

Parents are responsible for the protection of theirchildren. Unborn and small children are unable and not equipped to defend themselves against the schemes of the devil. As a result, God appointed agents to protect them and care for them. Again these agents are called parents. One day some years ago, the Lord opened up to me what I have since come to refer to as the **STRONG MAN PRINCIPLE.**

"Or how can anyone enter the strong man's house and carry off his property unless he first binds the strong man? And then he will plunder his house." (Matthew 12:29)

In this passage, Jesus is explaining how to expel demonic spirits. He says that there are different ranking spirits with which to deal. If you want to be rid of all the lower ranking spirits, you must first find their "chief," bind him, and then you can eliminate the others. The "chief" is called the strong man.

As I was studying this passage, one day the Lord spoke to me that the principle works exactly the same when the kingdom of darkness is attempting to invade your house. In the Greek language, the word translated "house" is the word "**OIKOS.**" This word in this context is not referring to the physical dwelling place, but rather to the family. **OIKOS** literally means: "the descendants thereof."

So when the enemy (the devil and demonic spirits) comes to plunder your house (OIKOS), he is after your family. His purpose is to devastate and destroy your marriage, children, and grandchildren. In order to do so, he must first bind the strong man. Who is the strong man of your house? The husband is the strong man to the wife, and both parents are strongmen to the children. Thus, in the areas of life in which the enemy can bind the parents, he has access to the children. The Lord demonstrated this principle to me in a very powerful way several years ago.

SALLY'S ILL-CONCEIVED SON

At an out-of-town seminar I was conducting, Sally came up to me with great concern for her five-year-old son, Billy. Billy was absolutely consumed with sexual lust in a very abnormal way, his mother reported. His mouth was continually spouting sexual obscenities. He knew all the latest sexual jokes. He devoured any type of pornography he could find. Sally told us that one day when she had left the room for only a few minutes, she returned only to find Billy stark naked, attempting to sexually mount his little one-and-a-half-year-old baby sister.

"This is not normal for a five-year-old even to be aware of such things," the distraught mother said. "I don't know where he could have picked up such thinking and behavior. He has never, to our knowledge, been around people who think or act this way. My husband and I are very careful about what kind of friends Billy plays with. He has never been sexually molested. Of course, now no other parents will let their children play with Billy. We just don't know what to do. He is a constant embarrassment to me. I can't take him anywhere, because I never know what he is going to do or say. I have to watch him continually at home for fear of his molesting the baby. We've tried praying for him, taking him to a counselor, and everything we know of, but nothing seems to help."

Sally's pastor was sitting with me as she described her son's behavior. The pastor confirmed that it was indeed as bad as she depicted and that they had done everything they knew to do. I didn't have any answers for them, so I suggested that we pray. As we prayed, I felt led of the Lord to begin to ask Sally some questions about the time of Billy's conception and early months in the womb.

As I began to query regarding the time of conception, Sally hung her head in shame and began to weep quietly. "I was far away from the Lord at that time," she responded. "As a matter of fact, I was involved in a very immoral lifestyle. The night that Billy was conceived, I was participating in a sexual orgy with several different men. I have no idea which one might even have been his father. This lifestyle continued for another three months or so, and then I gave my life back to the Lord Jesus. Since that time I have been walking with the Lord and have had no more involvement in sexual immorality. Shortly after Billy was born, I met my husband, who is a godly man. We have been serving the Lord ever since."

As Sally shared this information, the Lord quickened to me a very strange thought. Little Billy had been demonized by a spirit of sexual lust right at the time of conception. His current behavior was a result of the influence of that demonic spirit in his life. I then shared this with the pastor and the mother. At this point, weasked Sally to renounce all sexual immorality and lust in order to close the door which she had opened in her son's life. I then suggested that the pastor get together with Billy and his parents. Now knowing with what they were dealing and how it had entered, they should exercise their authority in Christ and expel the demonic spirit from Billy's life.

About two months later I was back in that same city again. Right after the meeting, Sally came running excitedly up to me. She reported that they had indeed met with their pastor and had seen Billy delivered from the spirit of lust. His life had instantly changed that day from darkness into light. He was restored to being a normal, little five-year-old boy, with no understanding of sexual things at all. Sally was almost beside herself with joy and just couldn't stop thanking the Lord for setting her son free.

This experience demonstrated to me the serious charge that parents have from the Lord as gatekeepers or strongmen in the lives of their children. Sally was bound in the area of sexual immorality, and, as a result, opened a door for her son to be afflicted with a demonic spirit even from the womb. This is not fair to small children who have no understanding of spiritual warfare and no defense against the schemes of the enemy. That is the reason why God made parents the protective agents in the lives of their children.

MARRIAGE AND GOD'S HIGH VALUE PROTECT CHILDREN

Because of children's vulnerability, I believe God gave protective measures in the law of Moses. For the ancient Hebrew people, He wanted to ensure that children would be blessed right from the time of conception. Identity of a child is blessed at the time of conception when two primary requirements are met: 1. The conception occurs between two people who have chosen to place themselves under God's authority through marriage. 2. The child is wanted, accepted, and received. A child's identity can be cursed at the time of conception when the child is: 1. Conceived outside of wedlock. or 2. Not wanted, accepted and received, or considered an intrusion into the life of the mother.

A marriage, (even among non-Christians) because it is an institution of God, creates a protective hedge around children. From a spiritual warfare standpoint, a child conceived outside of marriage is sitting on top of a pile of bricks completely exposed to the enemy. However, a child conceived within a marriage is enclosed in a brick fort. Some say, "You mean to tell me that there is a difference whether I engage in sexual intercourse with my fiancee five minutes before the wedding ceremony or five minutes afterwards?" There certainly is. This is particularly true if a child is conceived. In addition, there are several other devastating consequences to the couple, but these are beyond the scope of my topic in this book.

As a result of God's concern for the well-being of people, especially children, He established in the law of Moses protective measures that virtually ensured that no one would have to bear the devastation of having his/her identity cursed or of being demonized at the time of conception. Almost all cases of fornication and adultery (sexual intercourse with someone who was not your covenant marriage partner) were a capital offense. If you engaged in this kind of activity, you lost your life, for the penalty was death. This law significantly cut down on the occurrence of such activity in that society.

Until I understood the strong-man principle and the heart of God for children, I never could comprehend why God put such severe consequences for sexual immorality in the law of Moses. God's heart is to protect the identity of the children, not to arbitrarily and judgmentally curtail people's sexual enjoyment.

A second, protective measure that God put in that society was the high value and priority placed on children. The greatest curse that could ever come upon a Jewish woman was to be barren and have no children. Thus, again it was impossible to be conceived and not wanted. You couldn't be conceived out of wedlock, because the parents would forfeit their lives for that. You couldn't be unwanted when conceived, because everybody wanted children. They were considered a blessing and heritage from the Lord.

These protective measures were walls that God placed in that society to preserve the right image of identity and destiny of His people. Unfortunately, these walls are no longer in existence, even in much of the church. We have forsaken God's ancient paths. The results are that now I continually find people who have struggled all their lives with feelings of being a mistake.Oftentimes, in their parents' sight, they were. Many struggle with lifelong feelings of depression, fear, irrational anger, lust, guilt, as well as varied demonic afflictions. God never intended for anyone to have to bear these burdens.

RELEASE INTO ADULT IDENTITY

Not only did God place protective measures in the ancient Hebrew culture, but in virtually every culture of the world, including ours. We have simply allowed the walls of our culture to crumble around us, not realizing their purpose and significance. Almost every culture in the world has a way of releasing young men and women into adult identity. Our North American culture is almost totally devoid of this in modern times. In the ancient Jewish culture, every young man was initiated into adulthood through Bar Mitzvah. It was virtually impossible not to be blessed and released into adult identity at the time of puberty. You couldn't miss it. It happened to everybody. In our society today it would be rare to have a significant impartation of adult identity and destiny at the time of puberty.

THE KEY ROLE OF THE FATHER

I believe that at this crucial time in life the father is the key role player and has the voice of God for his son or daughter to release him or her into adult identity. When this does not happen, often there is a lingering question that remains on into adulthood, "Am I a real man, or am I a real woman?" Much of the sexual promiscuity taking place among teenagers is, in my opinion, a result of the lack of blessing by parents at the time of puberty as well as young men and women's attempts to prove to themselves and each other that they are "real men" and "real women."

In societies where there is a release into adult identity through blessing at the time of puberty, there is almost no gender confusion or homosexuality in adulthood. It is nearly impossible and even comical to imagine a Native American Indian brave who thought he was a squaw. There was such a powerful impartation of adult gender identity into the lives of young people in most Indian cultures that such a situation was unknown and non-existent.

Another result of not being blessed at the time of puberty is the feeling that in certain areas of a person's life he/she is still a child, although in reality an adult. It is not a rational thought, but only a feeling. I have talked to many adults who still feel like small children in some particular area of life. Some have thought that the feeling would go away when they reached age 30 or 40 or, for some, even 50 or older, but the feeling never goes away. When blessing has taken place at the time of puberty, it seems to cut in a healthy way an identity tie with the mother and release something on the inside to accept oneself totally as an adult. I have also found many times that this feeling is eliminated through ministering the blessing of God the Father even at a later time in life. This can effectively be done by the father or by a pastor or other significant person.

Since the father is the key role player in ministering blessing to his children at this vital time of life, it is amazing to me to check divorce statistics regarding the age of children at the time of divorce. More often than not, divorce occurs in a family right before the age of puberty of the firstborn child. This has to be a scheme of the devil to remove the father from the home before he has an opportunity to bless and impart adult identity and destiny to his children.

Even when a father misses the opportunity to bless a son or daughter at the time of puberty, this can still take place at a later time in life if the father realizes and understands the need. This will still be tremendously freeing and will have a powerful impact on the life of even an adult son or daughter. This was true regarding Ed and his daughter, Susan.

IT'S NOT TOO LATE FOR SUSAN

Susan was conceived as a result of an adulterous affair between Ed and her mother. At the time of conception, Susan's mother was married to another man, but she became involved in an affair with Ed. Shortly after the baby was conceived, Susan's mother divorced her husband and married Ed. However, this marriage lasted only two years. Not long after the divorce, Ed gave his life to Jesus Christ and subsequently became a pastor.

A few years later, Ed met a wonderful, Christian woman and married her. Over the course of the years, Ed and his second wife had four lovely children, all of whom loved the Lord. Meanwhile, Susan grew up with her mother and had only occasional contact with her father. Deep in his heart, Ed dearly loved his daughter, Susan, but it was difficult for him to totally accept her. She was a reminder to him of his past adultery and divorce.

I first met Ed and his family, including Susan, when Susan was 21 years old. Ed had taken the summer off from his pastorate to attend an intensive discipleship course at which I was one of the speakers. Susan had just given her life to the Lord about six months prior to this time and had decided to spend the summer with her dad and his family. She really hadn't known her father very well, and the relationship was quite strained.

When I first met Susan, it was quite evident that she had not received much blessing in her life. She was significantly overweight, wore her hair long, and let it cover her face most of the time. Rarely did she make eye contact with anyone, and usually she just looked down at the floor. She appeared like a scared little mouse who didn't think very much of herself.

During the course of the week, as I began to teach the material in the seminar, Ed was deeply touched. He soon realized that at each of the seven critical times when blessing was necessary in the life of his daughter, he had not been there for her. Actually, without realizing it, he had cursed her. Before he could minister to his daughter, Ed understood that he needed to receive ministry into his own life in the areas where his parents had not blessed him. This ministry followed later that same day. We told the seminar participants that the next day there would be opportunity for those with children there with them to pray for their children and minister into their lives. We instructed them as to how to do so.

Ed went back to his room that evening and sought the Lord about key times in Susan's life when he should have blessed her and hadn't. He prepared to humble himself, repent, ask his daughter's forgiveness, and bless her now. Susan was very apprehensive when the time came for her father's prayer for her. She had been hurt so much by him in the past that she wasn't sure she wanted to be there at all.

Several families had gathered all for the same purpose –to ask forgiveness of past cursing and now bless their children. Each family was seated in a private circle. I initiated the ministry time with a prayer inviting the Lord's presence. Shortly after this, I saw Ed drop to his knees in front of the chair in which his daughter, Susan, was seated. He began to speak to her about each of the times in her life when he had not blessed her. He had actually been used as an agent of Satan to impart his message to her. I could tell that it was a very difficult and humbling time for Ed. He spoke something like the following to his daughter:

"Susan, I haven't been a father to you. I've lived my life in selfishness, not considering your feelings at all." Susan began to weep uncontrollably at this point. Her father continued, "When you were born, your mother and I hadn't planned for you. We considered only ourselves. I know that I must have made you feel unwanted and unloved. But, Susan, God has shown me that even though we didn't plan for you, He did. You are no mistake. You are supposed to be here."

Ed continued, "And then when you were a little girl, and your mom and I divorced, you must have felt abandoned and unloved. You needed a daddy, and I wasn't there for you. Please forgive me. I was so wrong. Then, as you were growing up, I must have made you feel as though I was ashamed of you just for existing. I was so selfish. All I cared about was my reputation and my ministry. I didn't care about your heart. That was so wrong of me. Please forgive me."

"Remember on your 8th birthday, when I promised to take you horseback riding, and then I had an emergency at the church and never took you? I never made that up to you. You must have felt as if everything and everyone were more important to me than you were. That was so wrong. Please forgive me."

Ed went through his daughter's entire life repenting of the things that God had shown him and asking his daughter's forgiveness. Susan was weeping so profusely that she could barely choke out the words, "I forgive you."

After Ed had finished repenting, which took about 15 minutes, he then began to bless.

Some of what Ed told his daughter was similar to the following: "Honey, I know that most of your life I have made you feel that you are not very important to me or that you are even a shame to me. But today I want you to know that even during all that time, I loved you very deeply and just didn't know how to tell you. I have been so bound up with all my own guilt and shame over past failures in my life that I couldn't tell you how much you mean to me and how much I really love you. You can't know how many times during your growing-up years I longed to hold you close and tell you how much I loved you and how special you were to me. But I couldn't, because you weren't with me. So all I could do was pray for you. Then when I did see you, I couldn't tell you. Please forgive me."

Ed continued, "When you came into your womanhood, I never let you know how proud I was of you and how beautiful you are. God has made you a beautiful woman, well equipped with everything you need to be very pleasing both to God and to a man. Honey, I am so proud of you, proud that you are my daughter! Wherever you go, I want everyone to know that you are MY daughter. You are very, very special to me, and I love you."

There were many, many other things that this father said in repenting before his daughter and in blessing her, but they are far too lengthy to recount here. I noticed that as Ed was speaking, it was almost as if his words carried an electrical charge with them. I could literally see the power of God flowing through Ed to his daughter. It was the type of supernatural power jump I described in Chapter

One when a copper wire is aligned parallel with a set of overhead, high-tension lines. I was observing a miracle taking place before my eyes.

As Ed told his daughter how special she was and how much he loved her, she fell forward into his arms, wrapped her arms around his neck, buried her face in his chest and kept crying, "Daddy, I love you. I love you." When she emerged from her father's embrace, Susan was an entirely different woman. Literally, as different as a butterfly is from a caterpillar. A total transformation had taken place. As she pushed her hair back out of her face, there was a physical glow about her countenance, a radiance in her eyes, and the demeanor of a royal princess.

Ed had no idea before that week that he held in his hand the key that would change his daughter's life forever. Through later correspondence, Ed confirmed that his repentance to and blessing of his daughter that day had totally changed her image of herself and the direction of her life. Without realizing it, Ed had been sending his daughter the devil's message of identity and destiny instead of God's all those years. When the walls (God's protective measures in a culture) are only a few ruins, then even pastors and their families and flocks perish for lack of knowledge.

FREEDOM IS MORE THAN KNOWLEDGE

I have mentioned several times the seven crucial times in life when God intended to impart His image of our identity and destiny through parental blessing. Perhaps you are wondering at this point, "Is he ever going to tell me what are these seven special times in life?" The answer is: yes. I will list them for you here, but without any details of what to do.

1. Conception
2. In Utero
3. Birth
4. Infancy
5. Puberty
6. Marriage
7. Older age

The reason for not discussing here further details, is because we are a knowledge oriented society. Many people in the body of Christ are book and tape (knowledge) addicts. Knowledge, however, in and of itself, does not bring freedom or lasting change to one's life. Many of the things we are discussing in this book are issues of the heart, not the mind. Ministry to the heart must take place, not just knowledge to the head. It will not help you to know in your head about the seven times of blessing. You need ministry to the heart in the areas where there has been cursing and not just to know about blessing but also to experience it. (For more information on how you can participate in an **ANCIENT PATHS SEMINAR** in your local area see page 108 at the back of this book.)

You may say, "But I don't care so much about myself. I just want to know, so that I won't do any further damage to my children. Then they won't have to bear much of the pain and destruction that I have already had to bear in my own life." Of course, the truth of the matter is that you can minister to your children only out of the healing and wholeness in your own life. It's your life that shapes your children, not your knowledge alone. So if you want to bless the lives of your children, the place to start is to allow the Lord to touch your heart and bring healing and blessing.

When I first began to study this area and minister into the lives of others, the Lord clearly spoke to me that if I merely dispensed information without ministering to the hearts of those who were receiving the information, I would serve only to help further harden the heart. Remember Joe from Chapter 2, the one who thought that he had forgiven his father regarding the humiliation over the bed-wetting incident but actually had dealt with it only in his head and not in his heart? This is often true of many of us, particularly leaders of any sort. Often we are not even aware of heart issues, or how they impact our lives and families. This is the primary reason that I believe the Lord instructed me not to share here in detail about these seven times of life, because they require heart ministry.

In review, we have now seen that God programmed man to walk in His **ANCIENT PATHS**, which were meant to be protective walls for us. These walls are ceremonies, customs, habits, and laws which God established in society to ensure that people would receive God's message of identity and destiny through parental blessing. Over the past few generations, these protective walls, or **ANCIENT PATHS**, have been torn down and abandoned in our culture. Now, by default, most people receive Satan's powerful message of identity and destiny during their lives. Keeping this in mind, let's now turn our attention to more specific results in our society from the abandonment of God's **ANCIENT PATHS**.

The Ancient Paths

Chapter 5
ABANDONMENT OF GOD'S
ANCIENT PATHS

Before the Industrial Revolution of the 1840's, every child had a **FATHER**, a **FAMILY**, and a **FUTURE**. In fact, before 1940 in the U.S., almost every child had these same three "F's." However, in today's society, it is a rare occurrence when these three qualities are intact in the life of a child growing up. By the time most people enter into adulthood, they have endured countless experiences of identity cursing by those close to them. This builds up a very thick, protective callus. Although this callus is meant to keep out further hurt, unfortunately, it also serves to keep out love, even from God.

WALLS KEEP OUT LOVE

The picture on the next page depicts a man who has been deeply wounded and not blessed during his childhood. (A man is used as an example here, but the principle works equally the same for a woman.) When cursing of identity came, it deeply wounded his heart, causing him to erect a wall to block further pain. Unfortunately, this same wall meant to block hurt is indiscriminate and also prevents the love of others from entering his heart.

Love can be received only when a risk of being hurt is taken, and the protective wall toward another individual is pulled down. The wall that was meant to block future

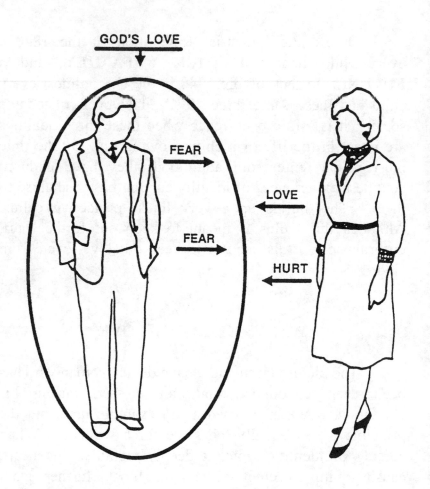

hurt, however, is really not a wall at all. It is actually a shell that also keeps one's heart from receiving love from God as well as from people. This shell creates a resistance to God's love, which is usually not evident to the one in whose life it is operative. The result is that the man cries out to God for help, healing, and love, and it seems to him that God is far off and not hearing his cries.

The truth of the matter is that God is trying to get His love through to the man, but, without realizing it, the man is resisting that love because of the shell around his heart. He thought he was protecting himself from the hydrochloric acid (cursing of identity) which had been poured upon him from people. Remember the battery analogy from an earlier chapter? This shell is the resistive corrosion on the inside of the battery cable ring which prevents the battery power from reaching the starter. The primary force which keeps the shell intact around the heart is **FEAR** of being hurt again.

The Bible tells us in I John 4:18 that "perfect love casts out fear." There is only one source of perfect love: God. God, indeed, is trying to get His love to every one of us. However, fear itself is the emotion and force that prevents God's love from penetrating the resistive shell and removing the fear. Thus, this man finds himself stuck. What can break the cycle?

I have found that the key lies in the understanding that, regarding the heart, as it is with men, so it is with God. Apostle John wrote,

> *"If someone says, 'I love God,' and hates his brother, he is a liar; for the one who does not love his brother whom he has seen, cannot love God whom he has not seen."* (I John 4:20)

75

So regarding the giving of love, if you don't love others, you don't love God, either. One day as I was meditating on this scripture, the Holy Spirit spoke to me that the receiving of love also works on the same principle. The man or woman who has an inability to receive love from people also cannot receive love from God. Why? The same fear of opening the heart to receive love from others will also repel God's love toward him/her.

The Lord showed me that the primary way that healing comes to the wounded heart is through taking what seems to be an inordinate risk. This involves pulling down the wall and opening the heart to people in a safe environment. The deep, intimidating fear that the devil uses to keep us from taking this step is the terrifying expectation of rejection, public exposure, and ridicule. Actually, when done in the right context under the anointing of the Lord, just the opposite is true. This is why the Bible directs us in James 5:16 to *"Confess your sins to one another and pray for one another, so that you may be healed."* Usually, if there is no confession to others, there's no healing. Why? Because the wall retained by the fear of being rejected and hurt still is intact, blocking you from receiving the love of people and God.

RESULTS OF HARDNESS OF HEART

The results of not continuing to walk in God's **ANCIENT PATHS** in our society are that now there are at least two generations of people whose hearts are hardened. They have developed thick, protective shells around their hearts. As a result, in the last fifty or sixty years, our culture has exchanged the value of **SELF-SACRIFICIAL LIVING** for the value of **SELFISHNESS**. Even some Christians have embraced this latter value. The goal of life today for many people is simply pain avoidance. Most people spend much of their time and energy trying to avoid further pain and to find someone or something to make them happy.

Unfortunately, most of the short-term solutions for removing pain are the very seed of long-term devastation and increased pain. Every day the heart devastation coming from the cursing of identity compels parents and children alike to make choices that further curse identity and create more destruction and isolation. The following data reveal the devastating, external consequences of having allowed God's protective walls to be torn down in our culture. Keep in mind as you look through these data that these are **DAILY**, not weekly or monthly statistics.

ONE DAY IN THE LIVES OF AMERICA'S CHILDREN

Every day in the United States:
  2,795 teenage girls get pregnant
  1,106 teenage girls have abortions
  372 teenage girls have miscarriages
  689 babies are born to women who have had
       inadequate prenatal care
  67 babies die before one month of life
  105 babies die before their first birthday
  27 children die from poverty
  10 children are killed by guns
  30 children are wounded by guns

6 teenagers commit suicide
135,000 children bring a gun to school
7,742 teenagers become sexually active
623 teenagers get syphilis or gonorrhea
211 children are arrested for drug abuse
437 children are arrested for drinking or
      drunken driving
1,512 teenagers drop out of school
1849 children are abused or neglected
3,288 children run away from home
1,629 children are in adult jails
2,556 children are born out of wedlock
2,989 children see their parents divorced

From: The Almanac of the Christian World, pg. 779, Edited by Edythe Draper, (c) 1990 by Edythe Draper, Used by permission of Tyndale House Publishers, Inc., All rights reserved

SHAME: THE RESULT OF IDENTITY CURSING

Having strayed away from **God's ANCIENT PATHS**, many of America's parents have lost and failed to teach God's message of identity and destiny to their children. The above statistics are the external results in society. God intended that each person He created be permeated with a sense of His **GLORY**. Glory can be defined as a feeling of dignity, great value of being, acceptability and legitimacy. Blessing of identity imparts God's **GLORY**.

On the other hand, cursing of identity delivers the opposite of Glory - **SHAME**. Shame can be defined as a feeling of lack of dignity, worthlessness of being, unacceptability, and illegitimacy. God's purpose in your life is to impart to you **GLORY** through blessing. Satan's purpose is to **SHAME** you through cursing. The city walls, which are God's ancient ways, were established by Him to protect your identity from shame and to give you His glory. Because the walls have been torn down, many of us, by default, have felt forced to protect our own hearts with a shell. As a result, we've lived for years with a deep, underlying feeling of shame.

WHAT IS SHAME?[1]

Shame is a deep, deep wound of being that is a result of the cursing of identity. Shame, as opposed to guilt, is a deep feeling of wrongness of **BEING**. Guilt, on the other hand, is a feeling of wrongness of **ACTION**. Guilt says, "**I MADE** a mistake." Shame says, "I **AM** a mistake." If I make a mistake, there is hope. I can repent. I can be forgiven by the blood of Christ, and I can change and not make the mistake again. However, if I am a mistake, there is no hope for me. I can change what I do , but I can't change what I am. Many people continually try to rid themselves of the feeling of shame through **DOING** things that they hope will help. They then become **HUMAN DOINGS** instead of **HUMAN BEINGS**.

Shame is a deep feeling of contamination, uncleanness, and of being uniquely flawed. It causes you to feel inept, different, and isolated from others. "I don't have what it takes to be a success," or "I don't belong; I'm not supposed to be here." When shame is working, you feel like you have to work twice as hard as others to accomplish half as much. When you look at peers, you feel like the only caterpillar in a butterfly world.

HOW DOES SHAME COME?

Shame primarily comes through the cursing of identity by important people in your life, especially parents. It is a result of rejection, scorn, ridicule, and unjust punishment. When identity is cursed, a fear of being all alone and not being taken care of is usually imparted. Shame is thus rooted in a deep-seated **fear of abandonment**. Identity is cursed, and shame is heaped on you whenever you have been held accountable and have been made to feel wrong for things beyond your control.

This was the case with Tommy one day in his third grade classroom. He had felt slightly sick to his stomach when he woke up that morning, but his mother insisted that he go to school, anyway. During the morning the illness continued and became worse. Tommy began to experience some diarrhea. At one point during the morning, the diarrhea became quite severe, and Tommy realized that he would not be able to wait until the bathroom break.

He politely raised his hand and requested permission from the teacher to go the rest room. The teacher, not understanding Tommy's situation, denied his request and told him that he would just have to learn to wait like everyone else. Tommy tried his very hardest to do so. However, after a short while, try as he might, he couldn't escape the inevitable. His pants began to leak. Soon a little brown puddle had accumulated on the floor under his desk. Then Tommy's worst fear came to pass.

A classmate noticed, began to smell the mess, and then saw the puddle. "Oooooh, gross!" she exclaimed so all could hear. "Tommy pooped in his pants!"

At this point, the teacher then came over to Tommy with a disgusted look on her face and, along with the rest of the kids, began to ridicule him. Finally, after what had seemed hours to Tommy, the teacher sent him down to the rest room and called his mom to come bring him some clean clothes.

This one experience imputed so much shame to Tommy that it impacted his life for many years to come. He had been held accountable for matters beyond his control and then ridiculed for his failure to control them. Before this time, Tommy had been a very outgoing, happy-go-lucky boy. After being severely shamed that day, he turned inward and vowed never to let things get out of his control again. He began to isolate himself from other kids, stopped trying new things, and became a very introverted, self-conscious boy.

SHAME COMES THROUGH PERVERTED FAMILY RULES

John Bradshaw in his teachings outlines seven family "rules" through which shame is imputed to children.[2] Every family has unwritten and inviolate "rules" which are communicated to the children at a very early age. In some families, the rules are godly and serve to set boundaries, impart security and blessing, and release God's glory to the family members. In other families, the rules are made to cover the shame of the parents and to make sure that their inadequacies are not exposed.

In the latter kind of family, the most wounding time for children is when they are the neediest. That is when parents who are filled with shame get angry, curse the identity of their children, and hold them accountable for circumstances beyond their control. My paraphrase and summation of John Bradshaw's seven family rules by which parents curse identity and impute shame are as follows:

1. Always remain in control of all behavior, feelings and circumstances.
2. Always be right and do it right. Never make a mistake. Perfectionism rules the family, and there is no room for a learning process. Everything must be the best and as it is supposed to be. Nothing can be tainted, spoiled, flawed or outside the plan.
3. When rules #1 and #2 fail, and things get out of control, get angry and BLAME someone. (Others, God, or yourself.) Children are held responsible for the parents' anger.
4. Deny everyone in the family five basic human experiences. It is wrong to:
    A. Feel. (Control all emotions. It's wrong to feel sad, lonely, fearful, or whatever.)
    B. Perceive. (What parents say is "right," period.)
    C. Need. (Always be self sufficient. Don't bother anyone with a need.)
    D. Believe. (Parents tell you 'Truth.')
    E. Imagine. (You have no right to imagine anything.) A lifestyle of denial and stuffing every "wrong" experience deep inside is established.

5. Always hide and maintain secrecy regarding anything wrong.
6. Never acknowledge a mistake or make yourself vulnerable to anyone.
7. Don't trust anyone. Relationships are erratic and unreliable.

WHAT DOES SHAME DO?

Shame results in elaborate "appearance management" systems to be put in place to hide the reality of life from others. It causes one to cloak and hide from others those things which are not perfect. Oftentimes this has happened within the church, under the guise of "holiness", even more so than among non believers. Since church people are supposed to be "holy," they are compelled by shame, not by God, to cloak and hide anything that is unholy.

One particular, striking example of this came to me as Bob shared with me about growing up in his family. Bob's father was a pastor in a very conservative denomination which had a particularly strong emphasis on external holiness. One day in Bob's early teenage years, his entire family was thrown into turmoil by the shocking news that his older, unmarried sister was pregnant. Bob's father was extremely fearful that if news of this were made public, he could lose his pastorate and be dismissed in humiliation.

With the daughter still in high school, the family chose to send her away to another city to finish the term of her pregnancy and go to school. After the baby was born, Bob's sister returned home, and, for the next two years, the family hid the baby so that no one would know that the baby even existed. Can you imagine the message of cursing that must have been imparted to that baby? "You are a mistake. You don't belong. You are such an embarrassment to us that we don't even acknowledge your existence."

Bob shared with me that when the family went somewhere, they loaded the baby into a box and carried her to the car that way so that no one would see her. When guests came to the house, one member of the family would have to take the baby to the basement to hide her and keep her quiet.

All this was caused by Bob's father's own shame and hardened heart. Because of his own shame for failing to control circumstances in his own life and family, he was unwilling to acknowledge truth and trust the Lord for the results. Instead, in an attempt to save himself from embarrassment, he chose to deny truth and heap great shame upon his own daughter and granddaughter.

SHAME VEILS THE GOSPEL

Another result of shame in the life of a Christian is that the image of Christ and the light of the gospel are cloaked to unbelievers, so that they are hindered from knowing Christ.

> *"But we have renounced the things hidden because of shame, not walking in craftiness of adulterating the word of God, but by the manifestation of truth commending ourselves to every man's*

> *conscience in the sight of God. And even if our gospel is veiled, it is veiled to those who are perishing, in whose case the god of this world has blinded the minds of the unbelieving, that they might not see the light of the gospel of the glory of Christ, who is the image of God. For we do not preach ourselves, but Christ Jesus as Lord, and ourselves as your bond-servants for Jesus' sake. For God who said, `Light shall shine out of darkness,' is the One who has shone in our hearts to give the light of the knowledge of the glory of God in the face of Christ. But we have this treasure in earthen vessels, that the surpassing greatness of the power may be of God and not of ourselves;"*
> (II Corinthians 4:2-7)

Shame causes an intense focus on self. Paul tells us in the above passage that we are to renounce the things hidden because of shame. Shame causes one to focus on the vessel of clay rather than on the glory of God which the vessel contains. Whenever great light is pouring forth out of the vessel of clay, the vessel becomes transparent, and all the cracks, nicks and imperfections in the vessel become visible. If a focus then comes on the vessel, fear of exposure of imperfection compels one to cloak the vessel to avoid exposure. However, as soon as the vessel is cloaked, the light is also hidden. The gospel is then veiled to unbelievers in this way, so that they cannot see the light and the glory of Christ abiding in the earthen vessel.

The Apostle Paul in the above passage says that he is not focusing on the vessel, but on the treasure inside, which is the glory of God. He writes that he did not come to preach himself, but Christ Jesus. So we see that shame causes one to focus on the vessel and then cloak both the vessel and the light, so that others are blinded and hindered from coming to Christ.

SHAME CHANGES THE FOCUS

One of the best pictures of this phenomenon of cloaking due to shame came to me as Karen shared with me a story of one of her first experiences singing before a large audience. Karen had a beautiful voice and a tremendous anointing of the Holy Spirit to minister to people in song. This experience occurred just when her ministry was beginning to be recognized. Karen had been praying for the Lord to open the door for her to sing in some of the churches in her city.

One day Karen received an invitation to sing for an evening service at one of the larger churches in town. It was very exciting to her, and she spent several weeks planning out the details of what song she would sing, what the Lord wanted to do that evening, what she would wear, etc. One of her friends, who was an excellent seamstress, even made her a beautiful, brand new dress to wear for the evening.

Finally, the day arrived. Karen and her family entered the church early to sound test and make sure everything was in order. When it was the time in the service for Karen to sing, she stood up and nervously looked out over the crowd of about five thousand. The music started, and as she opened her mouth to sing, the anointing of the Holy Spirit hit Karen so strongly that she was barely able to continue standing. She sensed tremendous power going forth through her voice, and as she looked down at those in the front row, she could see that many were weeping. God was wonderfully touching their hearts. She couldn't see much farther than the front row because of the powerful spotlights. God's power was so strong that it seemed at one point Karen could almost hear a choir of angels singing with her.

Then it happened. As she turned at one point in the song to look behind her, Karen noticed several of the ministers and male members of the choir turning their faces away from her and hiding their eyes. That seemed a little peculiar, and she wondered why they were trying not to look at her. Suddenly the reason was obvious. The beautiful new dress she was wearing was made out of a quite translucent material, and Karen had forgotten to wear a proper slip. She had not recognized the problem at home, because in normal light the dress was opaque. However, with the strong spotlights shining at her from the back of the church, Karen's dress was now totally transparent from the back side. Consequently, the ministers and choir were all seeing Karen as though she were clad only in her undergarments.

The moment that this understanding came to her, all Karen could think of was running off the platform. However, the song wouldn't be over for a few more minutes. She continued to sing, but instantly the anointing of the Holy Spirit left. It was as if someone had pulled out a power plug. The rest of the song was just as dry and devoid of life as it could be. After what seemed like hours to Karen, the music track finally ended, and she made her way off the platform, out the back door, and to her car. She burst into tears and prayed to God that she would never have to see the pastor of that church again.

Months later Karen could laugh about the experience as she shared it with me. This experience is a classic picture of the principle which the Apostle Paul is sharing in II Corinthians 4:1-7. When Karen began to sing, she was focused on the Lord Jesus and His ministry to the people. At that time, the anointing of God was flowing through her, and the Holy Spirit was touching lives. However, when the light caused her, the vessel, to become transparent, shame took away all her focus on the Lord, and, instead, she refocused on the vessel, trying to hide and cloak it. As soon as the focus came on the vessel, the glory ceased, the anointing left, and the image of God within the earthen vessel was hidden. This is a good physical illustration of how shame works, and what it does.

OTHER RESULTS OF SHAME

Shame often breeds hatred and unforgiveness toward yourself. It can cause you to shrink away from the Lord instead of running toward Him. This again is for fear of exposure and concern that the Lord, Who sees all things, will recognize your sin and inadequacy. Then He will reject you just as you have rejected yourself.

"And now little children, abide in Him, so that when He appears, we may have confidence and not shrink away from Him in shame at His coming." (I John 2:28)

When I first read this passage, I always thought that it was talking exclusively about the second coming of Jesus Christ. But then one day, the Lord quickened to me that He is coming to me every day. Every day I have a choice of running **TO** Him or **AWAY** from Him. This passage reveals that shame will determine which we do. Shame will compel us to run from Jesus instead of to him.

Shame also oftentimes results in various addictions and compulsions as the inner man desperately searches for something to alleviate the pain of having the identity cursed and the resulting feeling of shame.

Often there is a strong desire to be needed and to justify your existence. Shame tells you that you don't even have a legitimate reason for taking up air and food on the planet. The truth is, of course, that God created you and ascribed to you the value of the life of Jesus Christ. That is what He paid for you. It is enough for you to be a son or daughter of the living God. There is no need to justify your existence beyond that.

NINE LIES THAT NOURISH SHAME

Once shame is imputed through the cursing of your identity, the feeling of shame is retained in adulthood through lies which you believe. Some of the lies which nourish this shame are the following:
1. What I feel is wrong: (anger, hurt, loneliness, sadness, joy, etc.)
2. It is selfish and wrong to have a need or ask a favor.
3. It is wrong to express a contrary opinion.
4. I should never allow myself to make a mistake.
5   I can't go out of the house without looking just right.

6. When I do my best, it's not enough.
7. Men don't cry or express emotion. (Men)
8. I'm here only to be abused by men. (Women)
9. I must be a "good" person. Good is a coded word that actually means **PERFECT** to most people. When parents use that word regarding children, it usually means many of the following things:
    A. Never inconvenience others.
    B. Never embarrass or disappoint others.
    C. Never have a need or become obligated to others.
    D. Do everything perfectly the first time without teaching or practice.
    E. Let others see only what is practiced and perfect.
    F. Never have a critical thought of others.
    G. Never lose at anything.
    H. Never get less than an "A" in school.
    I. Do everything you are asked and don't complain.
    J. Thrive on instability, chaos, and stress.
    K. Remember only the happy times.

If you find, as you look through the above lies, that many of them have been sown into your life by parents or others, it is important to repent of believing them, tear them down, and receive the truth from God. These lies that perpetuate shame are what the Bible calls "strongholds."

> *"For the weapons of our warfare are not carnal, but mighty through God to the pulling down of strongholds; casting*

*down imaginations and every high thing
that exalteth itself against the knowledge of
God, and bringing into captivity every
thought to the obedience of Christ."*
(II Corinthians 10:4-5.) KJV

HOW TO RECOGNIZE SHAME WORKING IN YOUR LIFE

Many times when shame is working in your life, you have such an effective denial and appearance management system in place that you don't even recognize that your identity has been cursed and that shame is working. Some people consciously experience worthlessness when shame is working. This certainly is an identifying symptom. However, others can't relate to this feeling as much as with a need to be independent and self-sufficient. This is also indicative of the presence of shame's working. Some of the external manifestations that go along with each of these two indicators are as follows:

FEELING OF WORTHLESSNESS

1. Anger when circumstances seem to be out of my control.
2. Fear of emotion. Fear of experiencing feelings or getting out of control.
3. Difficulty saying "no" to people.
4. Fear of trying new things. Fear of failing.
5. Frequent depression.

6. Compulsive sin or addictive habit.
7. Need to succeed in order to be accepted.

INDEPENDENCE AND SELF-SUFFICIENCY

1. Isolation and difficulty making close friends.
2. Avoidance of getting into a position of need or dependence on anyone.
3. Great difficulty in asking for a favor or for help.
4. Being a much better giver than receiver.
5. Being fearful or uncomfortable as part of a small group without being either the leader and controlling the group or withdrawing and not participating in the group.
6. Feeling tolerated rather than chosen.
7. Having been a recipient, feeling a need to repay.

You can measure the degree of shame working in your life by the extent to which you will let others express love and care for you without having to repay them. This is you if you are one who will never let others give you a birthday party, or you suffer extreme embarrassment if someone gives you a surprise party.

In review, we have seen that God programmed man to walk in His **ANCIENT PATHS**, which were meant to be protective walls to us. These walls are ceremonies, customs, habits, and laws which God established in society. In that way, people would receive an impartation of God's message of identity and destiny through parental blessing at special juncture points. Over the past few generations, these protective walls, or **ANCIENT PATHS** have been torn down and abandoned in our culture. Now, by default, most people receive powerful impartations of Satan's message of identity and destiny which imputes the feeling of shame.

---

[1] Some of the material on Shame in this chapter is a summation and composite of notes taken by the author from a public address given by Dr. Sandra Wilson at the "Free Indeed" conference, Denver, Colorado, August 31, 1990.

[2] John Bradshaw "Healing the Shame That Binds You," Health Communications, Inc., Deerfield Beach, Florida, 1988. Pp. 39-40.

The Ancient Paths

Chapter 6
FEAR AND IDOLATRY

In the last chapter we saw that when identity and destiny are cursed in childhood, the result is that a self-protective shell is placed around the heart, and a feeling of shame is infused into the inner man. We also learned that the protective shell around the heart is held in place through fear. Fear is a very powerful motivating factor. The shame which is planted through cursing actually is a form of fear. Fear ultimately is the primary motivating factor that enslaves you to Satan and keeps you from experiencing freedom in Christ.

> *"Since then the children share in flesh and blood, He Himself (Jesus) likewise also partook of the same, that through death He might render powerless him who had the power of death, that is the devil; and might deliver those who through* **FEAR OF DEATH** *were subject to slavery all their lives."* (Hebrews 2:14-15)

When I first read this passage of scripture, I did not think that it applied to me. "I am a Christian," I thought. "I'm not afraid to die. I would just go to heaven and enter on into God's plan for me for all eternity." Then the Holy Spirit spoke to me that this passage does not refer just to physical death but also to spiritual, intellectual, emotional, or identity death. God began to show me that even though I am not afraid of physical death, there are areas in my life where the fear of emotional or identity death is active.

FEAR HATH TORMENT

When the fear of death is working in some area of life, that fear torments the soul. *"Fear hath torment,"* wrote the Apostle John in I John 4:18. And so it does. Fear pushes the soul out of peace and causes a man to forget about God. He then begins to work his own works in the flesh to attempt to solve his own problem and get rid of the fear.

> *"For the one who has entered His rest has himself also rested from his works as God did from His."*   (Hebrews 4:12)

Whenever the soul is at peace, a man is free to relate to the Lord and let Jesus work His works through the man. However, whenever the soul is out of peace, fear strengthens the shell around the heart and stimulates the flesh to find a solution to save the life of the soul which is being threatened. Jesus talked about this as a man's seeking to save his own soul rather than relating to God and trusting Him as source. When the fear of death becomes operative in the soul (mind, will, and emotions), the flesh goes to work seeking to find a way to "save" the life of the soul.

> *"For whoever wishes to save his own life shall lose it; but whoever loses his life for My*

sake and the gospel's shall save it. For what does it profit a man to gain the whole world and forfeit his soul? For what shall a man give in exchange for his soul?" (Mark 8:35-37)

Here in this passage Jesus is not speaking about eternal life - life of the spirit. He is talking about the life of the soul (mind, will, and emotions). We know this by the Greek word used here which is translated "**LIFE**." This word is the Greek word "**PSUCHE**," from which we get our English word psyche or soul. Had Jesus been talking about eternal life or the life of God in the spirit, the Greek word "**ZOE**" would have been used. (For a much more detailed explanation of this, see my book "Deceived, Who Me?")

In this passage, the Greek word "psuche" is used four times. Twice in verse 35 it is translated "life," and once in verse 36 and once in verse 37 it is translated "soul." Jesus is thus talking about a man's operating in the flesh and attempting to save his own soul life by eliminating the operative fear of death in his soul. The soul will seek to save its own life whenever tormented by the fear of death.

FEAR OF LOSING EMOTIONAL LIFE

The Lord first showed me how this fear works one time years ago when I was driving home in the evening. I was about two hours late and was feeling very guilty. Before I could even stop to think about it, my mind was making up a lie to tell my wife, Jan, about why I was so late. I was afraid that if I just told her the truth about my having simply chosen to continue talking to others instead of honoring my time commitment to her, she would be hurt and angry with me.

The fear of her anger was actually a form of the fear of death. It was a fear of losing emotional life within. Remember that the Bible tells us it is the fear of death that keeps us in slavery to the devil all our lives. How does this work? The fear of death causes us to harden our hearts and seek to save our own lives rather than trust God and receive His life.

In this case, because I was in fear of losing emotional life, my flesh had come up with a plan to save my own soul through lying to Jan. The long-term result of lying would not have benefited my life or my marriage. As I drove home that evening, the Holy Spirit began to convict me. I saw exactly how the fear of death was working to enslave me to the devil. The fear tormenting my soul had pushed my soul out of God's peace, and now my flesh had come up with a plan to save my own life. In so doing, I would have sown more seed of distrust into my marriage which would have been highly destructive in the long term.

Fortunately, in this incident, as the Lord convicted me, I broke through the fear and became willing to lose my soul life and let God be my source of peace. On the way home in the car, I repented to the Lord of the plan to lie, of the fear, and the underlying unbelief toward God. When I arrived home, I told Jan the truth and asked her to forgive me for not making her a priority in my life and not honoring my time commitment to her. Instead of becoming angry, she forgave me, and our relationship was strengthened instead of damaged.

CURSING OF IDENTITY RESULTS IN IDOLATRY

In the first chapter of this book, we talked about two key questions which every one of us must answer each day: "Who am I?" and "Where am I going?" These are the questions which determine identity and destiny in life. As we have said, God intended to give us the answer to these key questions. When, in adulthood, we continue to allow Satan to answer these questions for us through others, we are actually entering into idolatry. Any time we grant someone other than Jesus Christ the authority to tell us who we are, we have made that person god in our lives. We have granted that person a position that belongs only to God Himself.

If a relational message of identity and/or destiny is conveyed to me by another person, and I simply receive it as truth without checking it out with the Holy Spirit, then I have just made that person a god in my life. I have entered into idolatry. No one else loves me enough to be granted the authority, on an unqualified basis, to tell me who I am. No one else, besides Jesus Christ, has given up his/her life on my behalf. Jesus alone is uniquely qualified to determine my identity and destiny.

Whenever a relational message of cursing comes to you, and you don't check it out with the Lord but just receive it as truth, it will automatically stimulate whatever fear and shame are working within you. The fear will then push the soul out of peace, and the flesh will begin to work a plan to save the life of the soul and bring it back into peace. In this way, you become enslaved to the devil. All he needs to do to seize control of your thoughts, emotions, and actions is to find a pawn to even inadvertently send you a relational message cursing your identity. Until you learn to go to the Lord and check out the truth of identity messages coming to you, you will continually find yourself in idolatry. In this way, you are letting others determine your identity and destiny and are fighting in the flesh to save your own soul from the implications of those messages.

THE TAILGATER SENDS A MESSAGE

One day while driving my car, the Lord made this principle alive to me. I was traveling on a two-lane highway on the outskirts of Denver. As I glanced in the rear view mirror, I saw a car approaching from behind at approximately one-and-a-half times the speed that I was driving. When this car came close, the driver began flashing his lights at me. As he did this, I felt something rise up on the inside of me. A little voice said, "Slow down. Get in his way. Hinder him. Who does he think he is flashing his lights at me? He doesn't own this road." I slowed down a little and moved a bit more over into the center of the road, just to hinder the other driver from passing.

This action forced the other car to slow down and wait for an opportunity to pass. The driver positioned his car right behind me as though he were going to push me along. I found myself full of anger and hatred toward a man I didn't even know and had never met. At this point, I began to dialogue with the Lord. I asked Him why a simple thing like another driver's wanting to pass had so angered me. The Holy Spirit spoke back to me with a very strange reply. He said, "You are so full of anger and hatred, because you haven't asked Me, **THE QUESTION**." I then queried, "What is **THE QUESTION**?" The Lord replied, "The question is, `WHO AM I?'" He then explained to me something like the following: "When the other driver flashed his lights and came right up and sat on your bumper, he conveyed a relational message to you that he is important, and you are of no value. He sent you a message which said, `I'm somebody. I have places to go, people to see, things to do. You are in my way. Now move, you worthless nobody!'"

"When that message hit your heart, it cursed your identity and stirred up the shame, worthlessness, and fear which were already latent there." I argued, "But, Lord, I don't feel worthless inside." He continued, "If that were true, then the message would not have found a place of agreement in your heart, and you would not be fighting to disprove that message right now."

"Actually, the relational message wounded you, because your heart agreed with it. The hurt from this message stirred up in you the fear of being worthless, which then began to torment your soul. So your flesh went to work on a plan to make you feel better and restore peace to your soul. Your flesh told you, `Hinder him. Get in his way. If he thinks he owns this road, show him that he does not. Since he has exalted himself above you, just exalt yourself above him. Show him that he can't control you. You will control him.' Your flesh told you that if you do this, you will feel better. It will ease the pain inside."

The Lord continued, "You never asked Me the question, 'Who am I?' That is the real issue at stake. The man in the car behind sent you a relational message about you, and you simply received it. You never even bothered to check it out with Me. Now your soul is tormented by that message, and your flesh is fighting very hard to save your own soul life. In receiving that relational message, you entered into idolatry and declared the man in the car behind you to be a god. You granted him authority to tell you who you are."

The Lord then said, "Please ask Me the question." So I did. "Lord, who am I in Your sight?" As I asked this simple question, an amazing thing began to take place. God Almighty began to bless my identity. My heavenly Father said, "Son, I love you. You are precious to Me. You are worth the life of Jesus to Me. I am so proud to call you My son. Let Me wrap My arms around you and love you. You are secure in Me. No one can shake My love for you or your destiny which I have planned for you."

As the Father was speaking these things to me, I began to feel more loved than I ever had in my life before. I felt totally secure, safe, and loved. Tears began to stream down my face, and I sensed the presence of God all over me. All the feeling of anger and hatred toward the other driver completely melted away in the love of the Father.

Hatred and anger are rooted in fear. At that moment, I understood as I never had before, what the Bible means when it says, "perfect love casts out fear."

The Lord then spoke again, "Now that you have asked Me **THE QUESTION**, please forgive the other driver." It was now easy for me to forgive the man. My heart was absolutely devoid of any anger or ill feeling toward him. It had all melted away in the love of God. I quickly forgave the other driver and moved out of the way to let him pass.

IN IDOLATRY, FORGIVENESS IS IMPOSSIBLE

I learned an important principle in that experience with the tailgater. **IT IS IMPOSSIBLE TO FORGIVE ANOTHER PERSON UNTIL YOU HAVE ASKED GOD THE IDENTITY QUESTION AND RECEIVED HIS LOVE FOR YOU**. The reason for this is that your identity is always an issue when forgiveness is at stake. It is impossible to forgive someone toward whom you are still in idolatry. Unforgiveness is always idolatry, because it continues to authorize another person to tell you who you are and to send you wounding and hurt from his/her relational message.

If you have ever tried to forgive someone who has deeply wounded you without revoking the authority you have granted him/her to determine your identity, you know that it is impossible to effect real forgiveness in your heart. You must go to God and ask Him **THE QUESTION** first. Many have tried to forgive "by faith," which is just a choice of the will. But it never releases the heart.

By going to God and asking Him to answer these key questions, you are revoking the authority you may have unwittingly given to others to determine your identity and destiny. You will also then place yourself in a position to receive God's love which automatically casts out the fear. It is the fear that binds the heart and blocks true openness and forgiveness.

After moving to the side of the road and allowing the other driver to pass, the Lord then spoke to me again. He said, "You are missing many opportunities for intercession, because you continually let others tell you who you are. Then your flesh is busy combating the fear and shame working inside, so that you can't hear My Spirit's prompting you to pray for others." He then went on, "Suppose I told you that the man in the car behind you is someone I love very much. He is very frightened, because his wife is in the back seat of his car giving birth to a baby. There are severe complications with the birth, and this man is attempting to rush his wife to the hospital. He is afraid for the life of his wife and their new baby. The devil is indeed trying to kill the wife and the child, and I am trying to get them all to the hospital. You have been in My way!"

"I have been looking for someone to intercede in order to release My power into the situation. Now that I have your attention, would you please pull over to the side of the road and pray for this man and his family."

Once I understood the situation, my spirit was really grieved over the way I had acted. I realized what a powerful force fear is and how quickly it can motivate one to idolatry without realizing it. In whatever area your identity has been cursed in the past, fear will potentially motivate you to idolatry. Then you are looking to someone or something other than Jesus Christ as the source for your life.

> *"No temptation has overtaken you but such as is common to man; and God is faithful who will not allow you to be tempted beyond what you are able, but with the temptation will provide the way of escape also, that you may be able to endure it. Therefore, my beloved, **FLEE IDOLATRY**."*
> (I Corinthians 10:13-14)

There ultimately is really only one sin: **IDOLATRY**. Every temptation is rooted in idolatry. The way of escape in every temptation is to run to the Lord, ask Him the key questions, establish Jesus Christ as your source, and die to your own flesh's plan to save your soul life. Many Christians have been sorely disappointed waiting for God to extract them from their circumstance, thinking that this will be the way of escape spoken of in this scripture. Many have stopped short at verse 13 and never correlated verse 14 with the previous verse. Fleeing Idolatry and running to God is the way of escape that opens the door for God to move in your circumstance.

ASK FOR THE ANCIENT PATHS

Having gained understanding of some of the tactics of Satan in his destruction of our society and individual lives, I believe that it is time for us to reestablish and walk in God's ancient paths. There is no need for us to continue attempting to hack a way through the jungle with a machete when God has established a superhighway on which we could travel and much more effectively reach the destination. It is time for us to re-implement the protective measures which God originally established in our culture to ensure that we would receive His message of identity and destiny instead of Satan's message. Let this be the generation in which the present destructive trend is turned around. It is my prayer that our children might not have to suffer much of the pain and devastation that many of us in our generation have had to endure, and if the Lord should not return in our generation, that our grandchildren might not suffer what our children have already endured.

"Thus says the Lord, 'Stand by the ways and see and ask for the ANCIENT PATHS, where the good way is, and walk in it; and you shall find rest for your souls.' But they said, 'We will not walk in it.'"
(Jeremiah 6:16)

Let's agree together in prayer for the restoration of the ancient paths in our families and nation in this generation:

Heavenly father, we confess that we have not walked in Your ancient paths. We have allowed the enemy to tear down the walls of protection which You gave us. We do not want to be like the ancient Israelites who said, "We will not walk in it." Lord, we are asking you to give us greater revelation of Your ancient paths and we say to You that we will walk in them as You show them to us. Father, forgive us for not previously seeing and asking for the ancient paths. Lord, reestablish Your protective measures in our society and heal our land. I ask You to impart to me Your message of identity and destiny and to help me impart the same to my family. Lord, heal and restore my family members and others whom I have inadvertently or intentionally wounded through cursing of identity. Lord Jesus Christ, thank you for the healing power of Your blood and its in Your mighty name that I pray these things. Amen.

You won't want to miss
THE ANCIENT PATHS SEMINAR
(From Curse to Blessing I)

What is the Ancient Paths Seminar?

An intensive time of teaching from God's Word, followed by sharing, prayer and ministry in small groups. As teaching topics are brought up, the small groups, led by trained facilitators, give opportunity for ministry in that specific area of the individual's life, marriage, or family.

The seminar is conducted in a Thursday evening, Friday evening and all day Saturday format.

Seminar Topics Include:

Communication
    Recognizing different levels of communication.
    Resolving Conflicts.
Purpose and Plan
    Overview of God's plan and purpose for
        the individual and family.
    How to release blessing.
Identity and Destiny
    Seven critical times of blessing.
    Impact of lack of blessing or cursing of identity.
Curses and Blessings
    Steps to freedom from generational curses.
    Personal ministry.

Vision of Family Foundations International

Family Foundations International is a nonprofit Christian ministry based out of Littleton, Colorado, USA. The vision and purpose of Family Foundations is to help re-impart back into the culture of the body of Christ, those safeguards God planned which facilitate the natural impartation to people of their true identity and destiny from God. Without such, the devil has been allowed to impart his lies of worthlessness and purposelessness to millions of people throughout the earth.

Who Should Come to The Ancient Paths Seminar?

The seminar is for anyone desirous of lasting change in your life, marriage or family. Many times we see unpleasant or unhealthy patterns in our life, but don't know why they are there and/or can't seem to change. This seminar is designed to identify root causes and bring lasting change to these areas.

For a schedule of upcoming seminars around the world or for information on how your church can host a *Family Foundations Ancient Paths Seminar* please contact:

Family Foundations International
P.O. Box 320
Littleton, CO 80160
Telephone (303) 797-1139
Fax: (303-797-1579
Website: www.familyfi.org
E-mail: info@familyfi.org

Family Foundations Materials Available:

Books:
The Ancient Paths –Craig Hill *
Bar Barakah –Craig Hill
Bondage Broken –Craig Hill
Deceived, Who Me? –Craig Hill
Help! My Spouse Wants Out –Craig Hill
His Perfect Faithfulness–Eric & Leslie Ludy
I'm a New Creation? –Craig Hill
Marriage: Covenant or Contract –Craig Hill *
Romance God's Way –Eric & Leslie Ludy
Stepping Into Adulthood – Jeff Brodsky
You Don't Have to Be Wrong to Repent–Craig Hill

Audio Tapes:
Abiding Under Authority
Blood Covenant I & II
God's Principles of Finance
Identifying Shame
Jezebel Spirit
Living Free of Anger & Frustration
Raising Godly Children
Relationships Between the Sexes
Softening the Hardened Heart
Soulical Adultery
Supernatural Relationships

Courses:
Biblical Principles of Finance
Marriage Motivator

Videos:
Bar Barakah I-IV

*(Also available in Spanish)